WHEN IT
ALL
COMES
TOGETHER

WHEN IT ALL COMES TOGETHER

RIVA TIMS

CHARISMA
HOUSE

Copyright © 2017 by Riva Tims
All rights reserved

Cover design by Vincent Pirozzi
Design Director: Justin Evans

Visit the author's website at http://www.majesticlifechurch.com.

Library of Congress Cataloging-in-Publication Data:
Names: Tims, Riva, author.
Title: When it all comes together / Riva Tims.
Description: Lake Mary : Charisma House, 2017. | Includes bibliographical
  references.
Identifiers: LCCN 2016049799| ISBN 9781629985985 (trade paper) | ISBN
  9781629985992 (e-book)
Subjects: LCSH: Consolation. | Tims, Riva.
Classification: LCC BV4905.3 .T489 2017 | DDC 248.8/6--dc23
LC record available at https://lccn.loc.gov/2016049799

While the author has made every effort to provide accurate Internet addresses at the time of publication, neither the publisher nor the author assumes any responsibility for errors or for changes that occur after publication.

17 18 19 20 21 — 9 8 7 6 5 4 3 2 1
Printed in the United States of America

DEDICATION

To my children, Zoelle, Zachery III,
Zahria, and Zion.

I am blessed to be your mother. When
you are obedient to the will of God,
there is no limit to what God can do in
your life. My darlings, I am so proud of
you. Please continue in the faith. You've
already begun to see God's gracious
hand bringing everything together for
us. What a testimony of His love. I pray
that each of you will always testify of
God's power and love in your life.

CONTENTS

—— ✦ ——

ACKNOWLEDGMENTS

———— ❧ ————

THIS BOOK WOULD not have been possible without the love and support of several individuals.

To my parents, Fred and Rita Jennings, thank you for assisting me in this journey called life. You have been accessible in every valley season and mountaintop experience. You have been a priceless support to Zoelle, Zachery III, Zahria, and Zion. I will always be grateful for your devotion to family.

To my identical twin sister, Rena Jones, you are not only the best sister in the entire universe but the best church administrator as well. You have shared the load of ministry, and I could never repay you for all you have done. Thank you for being a true woman of God, never compromising even when things get tough. You have been a rock and a sounding board for me. I love you!

To Pastor R. Douglas, Roslyn, and Amiri Chukwuemeka, thank you for your love and continued prayers for our family and church. I know I can always call on you.

To Pastor Jerone Davison, thank you for being such a great friend and prayer partner. You make me laugh when

I'm on the verge of crying, you make me fight when I want to give up, and you are always willing to stand in the gap. Thank you!

To my Majestic Life Church family, you guys are wonderful, and I love you with all my heart. We are connected for the glorious purpose of advancing the kingdom of God. The Lord has allowed us to accomplish quite a bit in a short period of time, but there is much more to do. I am honored to contend for the faith with you. I want to extend a special thanks to the ministers of Majestic Life as well as to the armor-bearer ministry and the pastoral-care ministry. You all have been the church's backbone by seeing to the needs of the members and helping me carry out God's mandate for our church.

GOD, your God, will restore everything you lost; he'll have compassion on you; he'll come back and pick up the pieces from all the places where you were scattered. No matter how far away you end up, GOD, your God, will get you out of there and bring you back to the land your ancestors once possessed. It will be yours again. He will give you a good life and make you more numerous than your ancestors. GOD, your God, will cut away the thick calluses on your heart and your children's hearts, freeing you to love GOD, your God, with your whole heart and soul and live, really live. GOD, your God, will put all these curses on your enemies who hated you and were out to get you. And you will make a new start, listening obediently to GOD, keeping all his commandments that I'm commanding you today.

GOD, your God, will outdo himself in making things go well for you: you'll have babies, get calves, grow crops, and enjoy an all-around good life. Yes, GOD will start enjoying you again, making things go well for you just as he enjoyed doing it for your ancestors. But only if you listen obediently to GOD, your God, and keep the commandments and regulations written in this Book of Revelation. Nothing halfhearted here; you must return to GOD, your God, totally, heart and soul, holding nothing back.

—DEUTERONOMY 30:3–10,
THE MESSAGE

INTRODUCTION

---— ✤ ——---

HAVE YOU EVER reflected on life's unexpected moments and struggled to make sense of why certain things happened? Imagine dumping a thousand puzzle pieces on the floor—it would be impossible to figure out the picture by looking at the heap of disorganized pieces. Trying to figure out life can be as arduous a task as putting together an intricate puzzle. Life is filled with moments that are exhilarating as well as times that are disappointing. Making sense of the highs and lows can be extremely difficult. The saving grace for puzzle-doers is the picture on the box. Without the picture on the box, it would take forever to complete the puzzle.

The same is true of life. Conflicting life experiences are like disassembled puzzle pieces. With the pieces strewn all around, you can't see the big picture. But when life doesn't make sense and the puzzle pieces don't seem to be coming together to form anything comprehensible, we still can be assured that God is in control. He sees the completed picture of our lives even when we don't.

The Word of God says in Isaiah 46:10, "Declaring the end

from the beginning, and from ancient times the things that are not yet done, saying, 'My counsel shall stand, and I will do all My good pleasure'" (MEV). In other words, God knows exactly how each piece fits into the puzzle of your life. And He knows exactly how each piece fits into His master plan.

I believe you picked up this book for a reason. I believe a divine appointment has been set for you. God wants you to know that He is able to take the pieces of your life—the good, the bad, and the ugly—and put them all together for His glory. I'm a living witness. Seven consecutive years proved to be the most perplexing of my life. During that time I kept trying to figure out why I was experiencing so much turmoil. But the more I thought about my circumstances, the more frustrated and discouraged I became.

Well-meaning people would tell me they were amazed that I was still sane after everything I had been through. I can understand why they said that. In a seven-year period I found myself:

- Separated from my husband due to his infidelity (2007)

- Facing a grueling fight for my marriage (2008)

- Experiencing the end of my marriage (lawyers, lawyers, lawyers) (2009)

- Struggling to rebuild my life from nothing and sensing God leading me to do the last thing I wanted to do—launch a new church (2010)

- Facing unbelievable grief when my ex-husband died suddenly (2011)

- Denied any claim to the church my ex-husband and I founded (more grief) (2012)

- Having to fight for my children and figure out what was next (more lawyers, lawyers, lawyers) (2013)

Finally, in 2014, I began to see some light at the end of the tunnel, as I watched the church I started, Majestic Life Ministries, move into a new building. Up until that point, the puzzle pieces of my life didn't make sense. I didn't know how God could possibly use that seven-year season for my good and His glory. But I've since learned that what was puzzling to me was never puzzling to Him.

In my first book, *When It All Falls Apart*, I talk about the first three of the seven years. In this book I share what happened over the next four years to show you how God can bring it all together. God will redeem your brokenness for His glory. He doesn't intend for us to go through valley seasons and still strive and struggle, living in defeat. He wants us to thrive; He wants us to overcome. He wants us to take dominion.

When it all comes together, God doesn't just restore; He makes us better than we were before. We come out on the other side with a deeper relationship with Him, a greater level of authority in the Spirit, and an anointing that equips us to carry even more responsibility in God's kingdom.

If the puzzle pieces of your life don't make sense, if you feel as if your valley season will never end, take heart. I believe the scripture that says, "They overcame him by the blood of the Lamb and by the word of their testimony, and they loved not their lives unto the death" (Rev. 12:11, MEV).

I share my testimony in this book as a way of overcoming the enemy in my life and in the lives of others.

I experienced extreme loss that left me feeling fragile and broken. I was devastated by the infidelity that led to the dissolution of my marriage. I lost my place in the ministry my husband and I had launched, my source of income, some close friends, my home, my security, my trust, and my covering. But when it all fell apart, God brought me out of the pain and restored my strength, joy, and hope. He'll do the same for you. God sees all the broken pieces of your life, and He will bring them all together for your good and His glory.

Chapter 1

PUZZLED

———————— ∞ ————————

WEARING AN OFF-WHITE suit, I walked with my children down the aisle of the huge sanctuary. My heart was pounding through my chest, and I felt nauseated, but it wasn't because of the thousands of people staring at us. It was because the man I had married, the father of my four children, was lying in a casket at the end of the aisle. My eyes filled with tears as my mind raced with memories of all our precious moments together and the years of our love and friendship. It made no sense that he was now lying before me in a casket. How were our children going to cope without their daddy? I felt it couldn't be real. It had to be a bad dream. He was too young to be gone.

My ex-husband, Zachery Tims, was considered a general in the church world. He was known internationally, and his tragic death drew the attention of national media. The who's who of pastors, psalmists, and civic leaders from around the nation were in attendance at his funeral.

After my children and I took our seats in the front row, I sat there bewildered by all that was happening. I had been separated from my husband for two years and then divorced for two years prior to his death. Neither of us had remarried, and our four children kept us connected. My heart ached for my children as they sat so close to their father's casket. They had not been included in the planning of his funeral. I understood why I was not involved, considering we were divorced, but I felt it was wrong that my children ended up feeling like outsiders at their own father's funeral.

Instead of honoring Zachery, many people at the funeral seemed to be more concerned with letting those present know how close they were to him. He hadn't even been buried yet, and already it seemed people were jockeying to take over his church. Weren't they supposed to be offering words of comfort to his family and his church members? Why were they vying for position at his funeral?

One of the ministers beckoned me to say a few words. I had not eaten, and I felt light-headed as I stood up. When I walked up to the pulpit and saw the massive crowd, I felt my knees buckle. My heart was broken, and the grief was overwhelming. I stood in God's strength as I spoke to our children and honored their father's life. I know God put the words in my mouth because I wasn't asked to speak until that day, and I hadn't prepared anything.

I never wanted this puzzle piece in my picture. Zachery wasn't supposed to die so young. After going through a public divorce, losing my place in the church I had cofounded with Zachery, and having to start over from nothing, I wasn't sure I could take any more pain or the church drama that was already unfolding.

"God, what are You trying to teach me?" I wondered. "Didn't I pass the test of humility when I went through the divorce and lost everything?" Surely this was more than I could bear.

Over the next year, as my questions and frustration

continued to mount, I began to study the Book of Job. And as I did, God began to give me insight into my situation.

The Bible tells us God gave Satan permission to attack Job even though he was an upright man.

> And the LORD said unto Satan, Hast thou considered my servant Job, that there is none like him in the earth, a perfect and an upright man, one that feareth God, and escheweth evil?
> —JOB 1:8

As the story goes on, we learn that in one day Job lost his ten children and his wealth, and eventually developed painful boils on his skin. Job was clueless as to why the attack was directed toward him, but he remained strong in the Lord. During that painful season, Job made two of the most powerful statements anyone can make when going through a trial: "The LORD gave, and the LORD has taken away; blessed be the name of the LORD" (JOB 1:21, MEV), and "Will we indeed accept the good from God but not accept the adversity?" (Job 2:10, MEV).

I'm not sure I could have responded that way if I had just lost my family, my health, and everything I owned. Job had an incredible faith in God's goodness. Despite everything Job was going through, the Bible says he didn't sin. He stayed faithful to the Lord. Considering Job's response to his trial, you would think God would have been pleased and told Satan to back off. But the opposite stands true. Even after Job professed his faith in God, his suffering continued.

Wait a minute. Didn't Job just pass the test of continuing to honor and love God despite having lost everything? It makes no sense...yet.

For twenty-eight chapters (chapters 4 through 31), Job had

an intense conversation with his friends Eliphaz, Bildad, and Zophar. Eliphaz's theory for why Job was suffering was that God was punishing Job for hidden sin. Haven't we all heard that one? The moment you are down for the count, people come out of the woodwork with their opinions about your puzzle. People become the judge and jury when a person goes through a test or a trial.

After Eliphaz accused Job of being in sin, Bildad accused Job's children of being in sin. Then Zophar rebuked Job for claiming to be innocent of wrongdoing. Job's friends sure knew how to support a guy when he was down. Finally Job replied, "How long will you torment me and crush me with words? Ten times now you have reproached me; shamelessly you attack me" (Job 19:2–3, NIV). It must have been painful for Job to hear people who supposedly knew him well falsely accuse and attack him.

THE PAIN CAN MAKE YOU STRONGER

I can relate to Job's experience. When my ex-husband passed away, it had been more than four years since I had been excised from the church we started together. I had not set foot in New Destiny Christian Center since that time. Broken, weak, and deeply hurt, I quietly faded into the night, so to speak. After that point I was drama-free, and I didn't cause my husband any public scrutiny, nor did I seek anything from the ministry we launched. During that time I quietly struggled to rebuild my life and ministry, so much so that most people in our community assumed I had moved to another city or state.

After Zachery's death I couldn't believe the shade that was being thrown at me, especially through social media. Although generated by a small segment of people, the accusations were very painful. I was being blamed for our divorce and for Zachery's death. I hadn't been in his life for four years. I didn't even know the inner circle he associated with anymore. Why were they blaming me? Why weren't they blaming the yes-people who were around him during that time? Why didn't they criticize those who allowed him to remain in the pulpit knowing he needed help? Why didn't they point fingers at those who had been in his entourage?

I knew what it was like to be accused of things you had nothing to do with by people who had no idea what was really going on. I had endured the pain of people's opinions after Zachery's infidelity became public. So this time when the accusations started to fly, things were different. I was different. The pain was still there, but I was stronger because I had a frame of reference.

As I studied Job's story, I began to relate to him more and more. The more Job was antagonized and the more he debated his cause, the more Job became assured that God was sovereign. The more I sought God for answers, the more my faith grew and the more confident I became that God was in control of my life. I had faith that God would take care of my children, just as He always had.

Job's words rang true in my spirit:

> I know that my redeemer lives, and that in the end he will stand on the earth. And after my skin has been destroyed, yet in my flesh I will see God.
> —JOB 19:25–26, NIV

After a point Job began to realize that it didn't matter what his so-called friends thought of him because Job knew he was innocent. In the end it was about him and God. Job was sure that he would meet God as his Redeemer when his life was over. Job was humbled knowing he would be redeemed from all his suffering—if not now, then after his death.

Job's assurance in God did not bring his puzzle pieces together. He was still perplexed about why he was going through the trial. Job was in agonizing emotional, physical, and spiritual pain. And interestingly enough, the more Job humbled himself, the more brutal the attacks from his friends became.

Look at what Eliphaz said in Job 22:5–11:

> Is not your wickedness great? Are not your sins endless? You demanded security from your relatives for no reason; you stripped people of their clothing, leaving them naked. You gave no water to the weary and you withheld food from the hungry, though you were a powerful man, owning land—an honored man, living on it. And you sent widows away empty-handed and broke the strength of the fatherless. That is why snares are all around you, why sudden peril terrifies you, why it is so dark you cannot see, and why a flood of water covers you.
>
> —NIV

We know that God characterized Job as a perfect and upright man, so where were Job's friends getting these horrible accusations? What caused them to become so belligerent in their attack against him?

The irony is that Job's stance didn't stop his pain or answer his questions, but it drew him closer to the Almighty. We see clearly in the Word that when the members of the Hall of Faith in Hebrews 11—people such as Noah, Abraham, Moses, and David—were tested, attacked, or persecuted, they not only remained faithful to God, but they also drew closer to

Him. This is a pattern in the spiritual realm. When we go through tests, we run either toward God or away from Him. If we want to understand the puzzle God is putting together when He allows us to go through our trial, we'd better run to Him. He is the only One who knows where each of our puzzle pieces fit.

The more I got in the Word, the more I found peace. I came to know God as a vindicator and a healer. I was in pain after losing the father of my children, knowing that any hope of reconciliation died with him. His death made the end of our marriage truly final, and it meant my children would never have their dad to see them get their driver's license, graduate from high school or college, get their first job, or walk down the aisle on their wedding day. I couldn't stop thinking that Zachery was too young, too full of life to be gone.

I could barely cope with the grief, and I was having to watch out for vultures flying overhead, vying for a position at New Destiny. Yet I knew that God had taken care of us thus far, and He would continue to do so.

God Is Speaking

Job had a fourth friend present who had remained silent when Eliphaz, Bildad, and Zophar were accusing Job. Elihu began to speak in chapter 32 and did so for six chapters, Job 32–37.

> But Elihu son of Barakel the Buzite, of the family of Ram, became very angry with Job for justifying himself rather than God. He was also angry with the three friends, because they had found no way to refute Job, and yet had condemned him. Now Elihu

> had waited before speaking to Job because they were older than he. But when he saw that the three men had nothing more to say, his anger was aroused. So Elihu son of Barakel the Buzite said: "I am young in years, and you are old; that is why I was fearful, not daring to tell you what I know. I thought, 'Age should speak; advanced years should teach wisdom.' But it is the spirit in a person, the breath of the Almighty, that gives them understanding. It is not only the old who are wise, not only the aged who understand what is right."
>
> —Job 32:2–9, niv

Elihu, the youngest one of the bunch, had been sitting back, listening to the arguments of those who were older and supposed to be wiser, and he became increasingly frustrated. He knew that what they were saying wasn't the truth. I can say one of the best things I do is keep truthful people around me. If you surround yourself with people who have self-serving motives and agendas, you will get contaminated advice. My identical twin sister, Rena, always has been a rock of truth for me, just as Elihu was. As I faced one unwanted puzzle piece after another, my sister refused to allow me to have a pity party. She continued to speak truth over my life, which built my faith.

In his discourse Elihu rebuked Job for having the audacity to say that God was ignoring him (Job 31:35). Then he explained that God's way of speaking to us may not always be obvious. He may speak to us through dreams, suffering, and even angels.

> For God speaketh once, yea twice, yet man perceiveth it not. In a dream, in a vision of the night,

when deep sleep falleth upon men, in slumberings upon the bed; then he openeth the ears of men, and sealeth their instruction, that he may withdraw man from his purpose, and hide pride from man. He keepeth back his soul from the pit, and his life from perishing by the sword. He is chastened also with pain upon his bed, and the multitude of his bones with strong pain: So that his life abhorreth bread, and his soul dainty meat. His flesh is consumed away, that it cannot be seen; and his bones that were not seen stick out. Yea, his soul draweth near unto the grave, and his life to the destroyers. If there be a messenger with him, an interpreter, one among a thousand, to shew unto man his uprightness: Then he is gracious unto him, and saith, Deliver him from going down to the pit: I have found a ransom. His flesh shall be fresher than a child's: he shall return to the days of his youth: He shall pray unto God, and he will be favourable unto him: and he shall see his face with joy: for he will render unto man his righteousness.

—JOB 33:14–26

Many times we become so focused on what we are facing, because we are trying to make sense of it, that we miss the voice of God. That happened to me. God was speaking to me while I was in the midst of my grief; I just hadn't been listening intently for His voice. I began keeping a journal and documenting every dream I had. As I did this, I began to hear God speaking to me about my situation. At times He was warning me not to move in a certain direction. At other times He was showing me that He would bring justice in His timing and in His way. I didn't know it then, but with each word He was putting the pieces of my puzzling situation in order.

Elihu explained that although Job was innocent, he wasn't better than anyone else. God didn't owe Job anything for being righteous. That's right. It is our reasonable service to be righteous (Rom. 12:1). God doesn't need us; we need God.

Elihu reprimanded Job and their three other friends. He made it painfully clear to all of them that they were wrong in their arguments and that none of them were as great as they professed to be.

Let's look at Job 35:

> Does this kind of thing make any sense? First you say, "I'm perfectly innocent before God." And then you say, "It doesn't make a bit of difference whether I've sinned or not." Well, I'm going to show you that you don't know what you're talking about, neither you nor your friends. Look up at the sky. Take a long hard look. See those clouds towering above you? If you sin, what difference could that make to God? No matter how much you sin, will it matter to him? Even if you're good, what would God get out of that? Do you think he's dependent on your accomplishments?
> —JOB 35:2–7, THE MESSAGE

God is not concerned with your social status; God is concerned with your heart. Elihu explained that even righteous people have issues:

> Oh, Job, don't you see how God's wooing you from the jaws of danger? How he's drawing you into wide-open places—inviting you to feast at a table laden with blessings? And here you are laden with the guilt of the wicked, obsessed with putting the blame on God! Don't let your great riches mislead

you; don't think you can bribe your way out of this.
Did you plan to buy your way out of this? Not on
your life!
—Job 36:16–18, The Message

Elihu held nothing back as he spoke to Job. He pointed out
that Job may have taken pride in his righteousness and his
riches. Although God called Job righteous, he still had some
issues God was working out of him. When things didn't go
Job's way, he had the nerve to say God thought of him as an
enemy. I'm sure Job didn't realize that the root of pride was
lodged in him. Yet the pain and suffering Job experienced
exposed the issues that were hidden.

The Fire Is to Refine

Through my pain and grief, I was full of fear and anxiety.
I had lived four years as a single parent and had struggled
alone to rebuild my life. Now it seemed drama was knocking
at my door again. Again people I knew—and did not know—
were making me the topic of their conversations. Again I had
to deal with the opinions of people who had absolutely no
idea what they were talking about. Again I had to shield my
children from insensitive, undiscerning, and ungodly people.
The "agains" brought great fear and anxiety that I thought I
would never experience…again.

Through the grief caused by Zachery's unexpected death,
God was testing me. I began to understand that the more
you yield to God, the more He prepares you. God was
definitely preparing me for something great. He wasn't
allowing the grief and fear to destroy me, but He was using
them to strengthen me in Him. The fire is to refine us, not
to destroy us.

> In this you rejoice, though now for a little while you may have to suffer various trials, so that the genuineness of your faith, more precious than gold which though perishable is tested by fire, may redound to praise and glory and honor at the revelation of Jesus Christ.
> —1 Peter 1:6–7, rsv

Yes, God was strengthening me. The Bible tells us, "Count it all joy, my brothers, when you meet trials of various kinds, for you know that the testing of your faith produces steadfastness. And let steadfastness have its full effect, that you may be perfect and complete, lacking in nothing" (James 1:2–4, esv). That is what was happening in my life.

In many ways this trial felt like déjà vu, but it really wasn't. When I went through the first trial—when I faced infidelity, separation, and the loss of everything—I didn't know how to fight. This time I knew how to engage in spiritual warfare. This time the drama and gossip didn't paralyze me. God in His infinite wisdom was using this new trial to expose the fear and anxiety still lodging in my spirit. I had to choose faith over fear. This time I better understood God's ways, and I knew He was there even though I couldn't see Him or hear His voice.

I knew this because in the previous three years, I had discovered some very important truths.

God answers our questions in His time and in His way.

When David was hiding from Saul because Saul wanted to kill him, David was already anointed king. After spending years living in caves and in the wilderness, David asked God, "How long, Lord? Will you forget me forever? How long will you hide your face from me?" (Ps. 13:1, niv).

Have you ever felt as if God has forgotten you? Have you ever felt that if you hear another prophetic word about how God is working it out for you, you will burst with frustration? Don't give up. Many times the answers you desire are in the words people minister to you and that you read in Scripture. The Bible says, "Faith comes by hearing, and hearing by the word of God" (Rom. 10:17, MEV). There is power in God's Word, whether it is spoken or written in the Bible.

When God doesn't answer in the time you think He should, start speaking the Word over your circumstance. When you are obedient to God, every delay is in your favor. God is sovereign. *Sovereign* means "possessing supreme or ultimate power."[1] One of the songs I listen to during valley seasons as a reminder of God's faithfulness is Daryl Coley's "Sovereign." In it he sings that God can do what He wants because He's sovereign. God is God. He is subject to His Word and the principles He established in it. He does things in His own time, but He is working all things together for your good (Rom. 8:28). As Job discovered, God is the Creator of all things, and He doesn't have to explain or ask permission for His decisions. We must trust in the fact that God is good and all His ways are perfect!

God's answers don't always make sense.

The apostle Paul wrote to the church in Corinth that "the message of the cross is foolishness to those who are perishing, but to us who are being saved it is the power of God" (1 Cor. 1:18, NIV). Faith and logic do not always work together. When you are walking by faith, oftentimes you must throw logic out the window. When you desire to have increase, you give. When you've been hurt by someone, you must pray for them. When you're weak, God says you're strong in Him. Many times God's ways don't make sense.

If the puzzle pieces of your life are in disarray, please don't try to make sense of them. You will be wasting precious time. I encourage you to make sense of God, not your situation. Your life's puzzle pieces are complicated, but if you let them, they will draw you closer to God. The Bible says in 1 Corinthians 1:27–29: "But God hath chosen the foolish things of the world to confound the wise; and God hath chosen the weak things of the world to confound the things which are mighty; and base things of the world, and things which are despised, hath God chosen, yea, and things which are not, to bring to nought things that are: that no flesh should glory in his presence."

What a powerful scripture to stand on. God has chosen you even though you are in a weakened state. That makes no sense, but it doesn't have to. God is in control. Isaiah 55:8–9 says, "For my thoughts are not your thoughts, neither are your ways my ways, saith the LORD. For as the heavens are higher than the earth, so are my ways higher than your ways, and my thoughts than your thoughts."

God sometimes allows the pain to linger.

First Peter 4 says:

> Beloved, think it not strange concerning the fiery trial which is to try you, as though some strange thing happened unto you: But rejoice, inasmuch as ye are partakers of Christ's sufferings; that, when his glory shall be revealed, ye may be glad also with exceeding joy. If ye be reproached for the name of Christ, happy are ye; for the spirit of glory and of God resteth upon you: on their part he is evil

spoken of, but on your part he is glorified. But let none of you suffer as a murderer, or as a thief, or as an evildoer, or as a busybody in other men's matters. Yet if any man suffer as a Christian, let him not be ashamed; but let him glorify God on this behalf.

—1 PETER 4:12–16

Yikes!

This is not a popular passage of Scripture, but it does bring peace to know that you are not alone. Think it not strange that you're walking through a season of tribulation and spiritual warfare. You are not crazy, and God has not forgotten you. Christ can be glorified through our suffering.

Trials can bring us closer to God—if we let them.

Unless you have lost a close loved one, you may not comprehend the intense pain grief can cause to your soul. My heart was broken by Zachery's death. I learned from my first trial that when it all seemed to fall apart, trials can do one of two things: draw you *to* God or draw you *away from* God. I choose to be drawn closer to God.

I want to give Him my all, just as Abraham was willing to give God his all when God asked him to sacrifice his promised son, Isaac. Abraham's actions proved to God that he feared Him because Abraham did not withhold his only son. Isaac was on the altar and Abraham's hand was raised to strike him when God said, "Lay not thine hand upon the lad, neither do thou any thing unto him: for now I know that thou fearest God, seeing thou hast not withheld thy son, thine only son from me" (Gen. 22:12).

In this verse God made a profound statement: "Now I know that thou fearest God." What a vivid illustration of the way God uses seasons of testing to see how we will respond.

"And though the Lord give you the bread of adversity, and the water of affliction, yet shall not thy teachers be removed into a corner any more, but thine eyes shall see thy teachers" (Isa. 30:20). It isn't until we are tested that we know how we will respond. Will you give God everything?

Little did I know that Zachery's death was going to lead me into the refiner's fire for three long years—*three years!* I was in an unimaginable storm that shipwrecked me in a place of uncertainty and insecurity. But even though I was unaware of it, God had begun to lay the foundation for me to stand in His grace. In the next few chapters I will share unbelievable occurrences that could have destroyed me if I had allowed them to, but God used them to work things together for my good.

Chapter 2

THIS IS NOT
WHAT I EXPECTED

Aᴄ FTER THE FUNERAL the children and I were left to face a new reality. Our grief was deep, and it was compounded by all the questions that were still unanswered. How did Zachery die, and who was with him? Why was his body in the morgue for at least three days before anyone contacted his family? There were so many missing pieces.

On top of all the questions surrounding Zachery's death, New Destiny was telling me there was no will or succession plan. That sounded nothing like the Zachery I knew. When we were married, Zachery would randomly quiz me on what to do if anything happened to him. It was hard for me to believe that a man as shrewd in business as Zachery was would have left no legacy plan in place.

Because Zachery and I were divorced, I was not considered family in the sight of the law. Yet all my children were minors at the time, and as their mother I had a legal right to manage Zachery's estate. But out of respect for Zachery I decided to sign my rights over to his mother. I knew Zachery would not have wanted me going through his personal items, and he was her only child. So I never once set foot in his home after his death. Zachery's mother handled everything regarding his home and personal items. Little did I know, signing over my rights would be a huge mistake.

As others managed Zachery's estate, New Destiny members were beckoning me to come and comfort them. Even though I was no longer involved in the ministry, I was still the only spiritual mother many of them knew. But it became clear to me that some of the church's leaders did not want me involved in ministering to a grieving church family. It was déjà vu. After Zachery and I divorced, I felt like I was being ostracized from New Destiny, and the same thing seemed to be happening again. Church members who had no idea what was happening behind the scenes felt I had abandoned them.

I felt my hands were tied when it came to my dealings with New Destiny at that time. Not only could I not minister to the grieving congregation, but since there allegedly was no will or succession plan, I also couldn't ensure the church would release to the children what Zachery would have wanted for them. I knew decisions were being made behind the scenes, but the children and I were being given very little information. I had to believe God would bring to light anything we needed to know and protect the children's inheritance. In prayer God assured us that He was in control and was working everything out, but He didn't show us how He was doing that.

How many times has God told you that everything would be all right but not shown you how He would work things out? Our natural circumstances can look completely different in the spirit realm. When we don't know God's plan, we have to trust His character. "God is not a man, that he should lie" (Num. 23:19). If He says He's working things out, He is doing just that. It's like the old church folks used to say: even when you can't trace Him, you can still trust Him. Faith arises in the place where you are uncertain about your future but certain about the faithfulness of the One who holds your future.

During that time several ministry leaders called to tell me God was restoring New Destiny to me, and the vision God gave Zachery and me would continue through me. But God never gave me peace that I was to pastor New Destiny. I got the sense that if I were to return to New Destiny, I would be walking into territory God did not authorize me to enter. God kept assuring our family that everything would be OK. But again, He never showed us how He would work things out.

Something similar happened to the apostle Paul. God gave him a vision about a man he was to help, but God didn't show him how he was to meet the man. The Bible says, "During the night Paul had a vision of a man of Macedonia standing and begging him, 'Come over to Macedonia and help us.' After Paul had seen the vision, we got ready at once to leave for Macedonia, concluding that God had called us to preach the gospel to them" (Acts 16:9–10, niv).

After he received the vision, Paul immediately headed to Macedonia. Several days after Paul arrived there, he and his companions decided to go to the river to find a place for prayer. There they ministered to some women they met, including a dealer of purple cloth named Lydia. She and her family were baptized, and she invited Paul to stay at her house.

Wait a minute! Lydia was not a man from Macedonia.

She, however, was one of the first converts of the church at Philippi, which eventually became one of the strongest churches mentioned in the New Testament. When the word God gives you does not manifest right away, you must keep moving forward and do all you know to do. Paul easily could have become discouraged. He traveled a long way based upon the vision God showed him of a man from Macedonia, and when he arrived there, the first person he found to minister to was a woman. He may have been wondering, "God, what are You up to?" Paul knew God doesn't mince words; when God said there was a man in Macedonia, Paul would not stop until he met him.

Nothing—and I mean nothing—in my life turned out the way I thought it would. I was supposed to be a hospital administrator happily married to my accountant husband, Zachery Tims. I never thought Zachery and I would become pastors, but God sent us to begin a church in Orlando. So weren't we supposed to be married still, building the third phase of the City of Destiny, the cathedral? Weren't we supposed to be leading "a family church meeting family needs"? Weren't we supposed to be there for each milestone in our children's lives and grow old together? My life was nothing like what I expected. But as Paul did, I chose to press forward and do all I knew to do despite what the situation looked like.

After Lydia's conversion, Paul and his team were again heading to a place of prayer when a slave girl possessed with a spirit of divination began to follow them. Paul cast the spirit out of her, but her masters were upset because the girl made them money through her fortune-telling. Paul and Silas were severely beaten and thrown into a deplorable prison for casting the demon out of the girl. I am sure Paul was thinking, "This is nothing like the vision God gave me. Where is the man from Macedonia?"

During those uncertain months after Zachery's death, I felt I was in a prison with my hands tied, not knowing what I should do. New Destiny seemed to be in upheaval as a new pastor was sought. Members were being removed from the church board, and I was deeply concerned about the way the selection process for the new pastor was being handled. I loved the members of New Destiny and didn't want them to feel abandoned again. I felt I had to stand proxy for my children and for Zachery's legacy. I reached out to the church many times, asking to meet with the board and attempting to talk with the person overseeing the selection of the new pastor, but again and again I received no response.

It wasn't my desire to pastor New Destiny, but as the mother of Zachery's biological children and the cofounder of the church, I felt I should have been part of the transition team to find a suitable pastor. The members of New Destiny often were seen on the local news protesting with picket signs because they were so upset by the way things were being handled.[1]

A few friends encouraged me to sue the board of New Destiny for taking actions that prevented me from being able to step in and help New Destiny transition to a new pastor. My attorney set up a press conference for me to announce the lawsuit. I didn't sleep the night before. I always had held my peace until then. I had never publicly spoken against my husband or New Destiny. I questioned whether suing the board was the right thing to do. But if not me, who would have the courage to be a voice for the church and my children? The press conference was to be held at a local community theater. Still in shock over Zachery's death, I stood before the television cameras with dark circles under my eyes and my hair disheveled. I stood only by the grace of God.

At the same time my press conference was scheduled, Paula White released a press release stating that she would become New Destiny's new senior pastor. I didn't know how that could be. I had been told the church was looking for a married pastor, and on top of that, she was part of the selection board. My heart sank, but I continued with the press conference.

I spoke about the passage in 1 Kings 3 in which two women came to King Solomon to settle a dispute. The women shared a room, and each had a baby of her own. One woman suffocated her baby while she was asleep, and while the other woman slept, the woman switched her dead baby for the living child. The mothers went to King Solomon to have him determine who was actually the mother of the living baby. King Solomon gave instructions to cut the baby in half and give each woman a part of the child. The fake mother showed no emotion, but the real mother screamed and told the king to give the baby to the other woman. Because the real mother loved her child, she would have rather seen the child alive with someone else than dead with her.

I wanted what God birthed through Zachery and me to live, and to do that I felt I needed to be a voice for New Destiny and oppose the board. New Destiny's legal team challenged my lawsuit, saying it was inadmissible because I signed documents during my marital settlement stating I would never sue New Destiny. Of course, that was based on Zachery's still being alive and pastor of New Destiny. My attorney felt we could take the challenge. I didn't want it to seem like a fight between Paula White and me or between New Destiny and me. I wanted only to make the board abide by the bylaws. So I ended the lawsuit and prayed that it at least brought some awareness of what was happening behind the scenes.

Many people commended me for taking a stand and getting the word out. But just as many people thought I should have kept my mouth shut and just let things be. I felt I needed to do something, and I was glad I did so. Unfortunately I also felt my efforts only pushed me further into the prison of grief and the emotional heaviness of Zachery's death. It was a "midnight" experience.

AT MIDNIGHT...

In Acts 16 Paul and Silas are in jail after having been arrested for casting a demon out of the slave girl who had been telling fortunes. They had been beaten and put in the inner chamber of the prison, with iron rods fastened around their legs. And this was happening because they answered God's call to go to Macedonia!

They could have had a pity party. They could have complained to God about their situation. But instead, the Bible says, "At midnight Paul and Silas prayed, and sang praises unto God: and the prisoners heard them" (Acts 16:25).

Did you notice that both Paul and Silas prayed and sang praises to God? It's easy to miss that fact. They came into agreement in the midst of death, prison, and suffering. Silas easily could have said, "Shut up, Paul. You and your so-called visions got us into this mess." Remember, they had gone to Macedonia to find "the man." Yet they had found only a woman named Lydia, a demon-possessed fortune-teller, and a prison cell. But God brought Paul the right companion to face what was in store for them in Macedonia.

During my spiritual prison experience with the board of

New Destiny I had great cellmates. The ministry I launched, Majestic Life, was growing steadily, and the foundation was healthy and strong. We were, and still are, a team-based ministry with no celebrities but Jesus. Majestic Life's leadership and members were very supportive during this time. I was lifted up in prayer by my church's leaders and my pastoral friends Bishop Stanley and Dee Williams, and Bishop I. V. and Bridget Hilliard. Because of these godly friendships I felt supported and validated during this time. God brings the right people at the right time, but the enemy will try to get you to connect with the wrong people. When you're facing a midnight experience, surround yourself with people who will pray with you and lift you up.

Midnight symbolizes your darkest hour. It's that time when you feel defeated or lost, rejected or abused, or just plain hopeless with your back against the wall. It's when you're bound by depression, addiction, or maybe isolation. Midnight seasons are usually when things don't add up, when you cannot see how God can make anything beautiful out of your situation. Midnight is when you realize you cannot change or fix the circumstance, and you give God permission to put you on His potter's wheel to reshape your puzzle piece to fit His plan for you. Now you may be shaped like a small circle, and your assignment is to fit in a large square. It's on the potter's wheel that God will increase your capacity as He adds to you. At first you may feel the increase is too much for you, but God knows just how much you can bear.

I felt that way when God called me to start another church. I saw myself as a small circle, but God knew He had created me to be a large square. On God's potter's wheel He increased my anointing and my stamina to pastor a new work. In the same way, I also have seen God decrease a large rectangle into a square. When God decreases you, it can be to remove the pride, arrogance, or self-reliance that can keep you from fulfilling His plan for your life. Although the adding to and cutting away can be painful, it is effective for positioning you exactly where you need to be to accomplish His will.

At midnight Paul and Silas found themselves in prison. That's hardly where they expected to be. They were men of God, and they found themselves in the midst of criminals in a dark dungeon. Who would have thought God's plan would have led them there? But notice that when Paul and Silas had their backs against the wall, they praised God. That's how they chose to respond to an impossible situation.

The vision the Lord gave them led them to Macedonia. Their obedience and good deeds landed them in prison. When they could have complained or gotten depressed, they chose to praise the Lord. And they didn't do it quietly in their hearts. The Bible says the other prisoners heard them praise God. What a testimony! Can you imagine what the other prisoners must have been thinking? The other prisoners were experiencing the same darkness, hunger, and stench as Paul and Silas. They must have wondered how Paul and Silas could be praising God.

People are watching how you respond in your darkest hour. Be an example of a true worshipper. God will use worshippers to set at liberty those who are held captive. So I determined that even in my midnight hour, though I felt imprisoned by uncertainty and grief, my disposition would remain one of prayer and praise.

At one point there was an issue with the children's inheritance because New Destiny claimed there was no will. As a result, New Destiny would not release anything to the children. Zachery's mother was trying her best to handle everything, but unfortunately it became a big mess. I signed my rights over to Zachery's mother out of respect for him and his mother. But I could see a storm brewing, and now I had no authority to do anything.

I felt overwhelming pressure. My children were minors, and they were looking to me to stand up for them. I wondered what Zachery would do in this situation. My hands were tied. We were divorced; therefore I had no legal authority. But someone needed to be a voice for my children. I surrounded myself with precious people of like faith. We continued to glorify God in the midst of the battle. I knew that God was in control. I didn't want to fight anymore, but I had to put on the whole armor of God and stand. Prayer and praise were the weapons I used daily. My cellmates were mature enough to do the same. The situation was dark, and I felt helpless, but I knew God was working on things we could not see.

Little did I know people were observing me from afar. My worship wasn't simply a song I sang in church; it was my attitude and my actions. Majestic Life members and former New Destiny members were observing my response. My children were watching me. And God was setting the stage to manifest His glory.

In that Macedonian prison cell while Paul and Silas were praising God:

> Suddenly there was such a violent earthquake that the foundations of the prison were shaken. At once all the prison doors flew open, and everyone's chains came loose. The jailer woke up, and when he saw the prison doors open, he drew his sword and was about to kill himself because he thought the prisoners had escaped. But Paul shouted, "Don't

harm yourself! We are all here!" The jailer called for lights, rushed in and fell trembling before Paul and Silas. He then brought them out and asked, "Sirs, what must I do to be saved?"

—Acts 16:26–30, niv

The earthquake revealed Paul's assignment. The man from Macedonia in Paul's vision was the jailer! Paul received a vision from the Lord, but God didn't tell him about the stops he would have to make along the way. Paul had to meet Lydia, the dealer of purple cloth, and Paul had to meet the girl with the spirit of divination. Paul also had to be beaten and thrown into jail because that's how he would encounter his assignment. God gave Paul the vision, but He did not give Paul every step of the journey.

You may be in the middle of your journey and feeling the pressure. You may be thinking that where you are in life today is not where you imagined you would be. Years ago I heard the late great Myles Munroe say that if what you see is not what you saw (your vision), then what you see is only temporary. So that means you must press forward and not give up. God will manifest His glory, and everything will make sense eventually.

The earthquake was not so Paul and Silas could be released from the prison because when the jailer rushed in, Paul told him to do himself no harm because they were all there. The prisoners remained in the unlocked cells because there was a greater purpose in the earthquake. God desired for the jailer and his family to find salvation.

An earthquake is a sudden and violent shaking of the ground, sometimes causing great destruction.[2] The operative word in this definition and in Acts 16:26 (kjv) is *sudden.*

When an earthquake occurs, you don't have much time to brace yourself, and you will not have control over your surroundings. The combination of suddenness and violence creates a frightening scenario. Zachery's death was a sudden and violent force that turned many people's worlds upside down and inside out. My children went to bed one night with a dad, and the next day they were without him. New Destiny members came to church on a Sunday morning expecting to see their pastor, and he was not there.

The man I was married to for fifteen years and with whom I had four children was never coming back. The ministry we built together was without a shepherd, and I was being pulled on to bring comfort and answers while in deep grief. I had been through several spiritual earthquakes in the previous four years, but none of them reached the magnitude on the Richter scale of this earthquake.

Yet God in His sovereignty was orchestrating His will. He would prove Himself to be our refuge. New Destiny had an insurance policy that named me as beneficiary. I had no idea it even existed. Through the earthquake God manifested His supernatural provision for my children and me. This may sound weird, but we felt as though Zachery was somehow looking out for us. With the resources from the insurance policy, I was able to hire an attorney and get every document signed to release the children's inheritance.

God also used the earthquake to reveal to me part of my assignment. I realized that I wasn't supposed to just go with the flow and follow the popular ministers' code of conduct. I had to stand for truth, and when I did, God exposed the agenda of those who were seeking selfish gain.

God restored Paul after his midnight experience too. The Bible says the jailer "took them the same hour of the night, and washed their stripes; and was baptized, he and all his, straightway. And when he had brought them into his house, he set meat before them, and rejoiced, believing in God with all his house. And when it was day, the magistrates sent the serjeants, saying, Let those men go. And the keeper of the prison told this saying to Paul, The magistrates have sent to let you go: now therefore depart, and go in peace" (Acts 16:33–36).

God prepared a table for Paul and Silas in the presence of their enemies. The same person who beat Paul and Silas cleaned their wounds and prepared food for them to eat. Your biggest enemy can become your biggest supporter. I believe that is why the Lord says vengeance belongs to Him. Oftentimes God is just gathering all the pieces to set the stage for the miracle. The earthquake after Zachery's death exposed people's motives and agendas. God was revealing the true picture. And when the truth was revealed, people who had rejected me became my supporters.

Interestingly God didn't let those who had mistreated Paul and Silas redeem them privately.

> But Paul said unto them, They have beaten us openly uncondemned, being Romans, and have cast us into prison; and now do they thrust us out privily? nay verily; but let them come themselves and fetch us out. And the serjeants told these words unto the magistrates: and they feared, when they heard that they were Romans. And they came and besought them, and brought them out, and desired them to depart out of the city. And they went out of the prison, and entered into the house of Lydia: and

when they had seen the brethren, they comforted
them, and departed.

—ACTS 16:37–40

If you have ever been humiliated publicly, you know how
painful and embarrassing it can be. The Bible says the magistrates treated Paul and Silas with great disrespect when
they were thrown in jail, not knowing they were Roman
citizens. After the earthquake the magistrates wanted Paul
and Silas to leave quietly. But Paul made it clear that they
accused them publicly and they would vindicate them publicly. Yes sir!

Roman citizens had special privileges and by law could
not be treated poorly. The magistrates could have been in
major trouble for assaulting Paul and Silas. You as a believer
also have special privileges as a kingdom citizen, and the
enemy is not allowed to assault you whenever he pleases.

Unsolicited by me, many people contacted me to apol-
ogize for what they initially thought or said about me. I
had no idea the things most of them said. Had I known, it
would have crushed me. God protected me and vindicated
me. Glory to God! He publicly vindicated me by revealing
the truth.

GOD WILL REDEEM THE TIME

It is amazing how God can change things in an instant. What
could have easily taken months or even years changed suddenly through God's miraculous earthquake, and Paul and
Silas were released from prison to carry out their assignment.

God said in Isaiah 61:7, "Instead of your shame you will
receive a double portion, and instead of disgrace you will
rejoice in your inheritance. And so you will inherit a double

portion in your land, and everlasting joy will be yours" (NIV). This is a powerful verse to stand on. Paul and Silas were vindicated, and God turned their shame into a major victory that brought Him glory.

One of my church members has a past riddled with bad decisions. She committed her life to the Lord, and as a result, she was able to see beyond her past and recognize her value in God. She decided to run for a seat on the city commission. Unfortunately the mistakes in her past were now relentlessly brought to the forefront in the news media. Though humiliated, she continued to campaign. We stood on Isaiah 61:7, and praise God, she won! Her opponents failed to realize that many of the voters also had made mistakes. They voted for my church member because it gave them hope that they could overcome their past also. It was such a powerful testimony of God's redeeming power.

God says in Joel 2:25–26: "And I will restore to you the years that the locust hath eaten, the cankerworm, and the caterpiller, and the palmerworm, my great army which I sent among you. And ye shall eat in plenty, and be satisfied, and praise the name of the LORD your God, that hath dealt wondrously with you: and my people shall never be ashamed." It is impossible in the natural for years literally to be restored. We cannot travel back in time and get a do-over. But the locusts in Joel 2:25 did not eat the actual years; they ate the harvests from those years.

What God is saying here is He will restore the lost blessings, the lost harvests, just as if the locusts had never come. That's how powerful our God is. He knows how to make up the lost time and get us where we need to be. Even if we were the cause of those lost or wasted years, He is merciful enough to give us another chance. And I've learned something else about God's redeeming power. Not only does He restore, but He also can do it in double time. What we have accomplished in ministry in the last seven years easily could have taken fifteen years. In one year—or even in one day—God can bring something to pass in your life that makes up for ten lost years. Nothing is too hard for the Lord.

Despite a divorce, years of addiction, legal battles, or health crises, God can still get you where you're supposed to be. That's what happened with my church member. In one day God took her from humiliation and disgrace to rejoicing in her blessings as an elected official. God did the impossible. He redeemed the time and used the situation to propel her toward her destiny.

God wants to—and will—redeem the time in your life. The only thing that can stop Him from doing so is you! As a pastor I have seen countless people hit brick walls in their relationships, finances, and health because they took their focus off the Lord. But the ones who kept their eyes on Jesus maintained their joy, and recovered or rebounded exponentially.

In Joel 2, when God promised to restore the years the locusts had eaten, He was speaking to a nation that had drifted away from Him. His promise was dependent on the people repenting and turning to Him with their whole hearts. Then He would restore what they had lost, and all the surrounding nations would take note. If you will turn your heart to the Lord and focus on Him and His will for you instead of seeking vengeance, playing the blame game, wallowing in shame, or thinking nothing will ever change, God will be able to show Himself strong on your behalf too.

To give God free rein to redeem the time in your life, remember these principles:

Watch for the opportunities God brings during your trial.

Ephesians 5:15–16 tells us, "See then that ye walk circumspectly, not as fools, but as wise, redeeming the time, because the days are evil." And Colossians 4:5 says to "walk in wisdom toward them that are without, redeeming the time." The word translated "redeeming" in Ephesians 5:16 and Colossians 4:5 can mean buying up or purchasing something.[3] And the word *time* in these verses is not the Greek word *chronos*, which refers to clock time (hours, minutes, and seconds). It is the Greek word *kairos*, which refers to God's set time to accomplish a particular thing.[4]

Tomorrow we will have another twenty-four hours, but we may not have the same opportunities we have today. Often we look at hardships and persecution as the end of everything. But even in our trials God will create strategic opportunities that He will use to redeem what we've lost.

Consider the example of the widow of Zarephath. Because of a severe drought, she and her son were starving. Her plan was to make one last meal and then wait to die. But God had a plan to get His *super* to her *natural*. He had commanded the prophet Elijah to go to the widow, saying, "Behold, I have commanded a widow woman there to sustain thee" (1 Kings 17:9).

When the prophet arrived, he asked the widow to make him a little cake. She told him her plan to make something for herself and her son and then wait to die. And Elijah replied: "Fear not; go and do as thou hast said: but make me thereof a little cake first, and bring it unto me, and after make for thee and for thy son. For thus saith the LORD God of Israel, The barrel of meal shall not waste, neither shall the cruse of oil fail, until the day that the LORD sendeth rain upon the earth" (1 Kings 17:13–14).

The widow trusted God's word to her and did as the prophet said, and she, Elijah, and her son ate many days. "The barrel of meal did not run out, nor did the jar of oil empty, according to the word of the LORD, which He spoke by Elijah" (1 Kings 17:16, MEV). Because the widow was willing to seize the opportunity God presented to her when she was in the middle of her trial, God was able to multiply her resources and give her more than enough in the middle of a famine.

In some ways I felt like the widow woman. After Zachery's death I found myself simply accepting what was being dealt to me and not putting up much resistance. I wasn't afraid to fight, but I was battle-weary. I felt that people, especially attorneys, were taking advantage of me. And without realizing it, I became passive in my warfare and began to walk in complacency and rejection.

I finally snapped out of it while I was on a business trip in Las Vegas. I caught a taxi to get to the conference, and while we were en route, the taxi driver said he didn't know how to get to the location. So he drove around the property of the airport and charged me twenty-five dollars to return me to the terminal—and I paid him. I sat at the airport and sobbed, thinking, "What is wrong with me? Why did I pay that con artist taxi driver?"

I realized I had been cosigning the enemy's lie that I was a victim instead of boldly resisting my opposition. I had all but forgotten the scripture that says the kingdom of God "suffereth violence, and the violent take it by force" (Matt. 11:12). Instead of becoming passive, which is easy to do when we're feeling weak, I needed to see my trial as an opportunity to stand in faith to take back everything the devil stole from me. God gave the children of Israel land to inhabit, but before they could enter in, there were giants that needed to be dispossessed. Increase awaited the children of Israel, but they had to overcome the giants. God wants us to stand boldly against every giant in our lives.

You also may feel battle-fatigued. You may feel as if you're in a famine. You may feel time is running out. But be encouraged. God has the power to bring you out of your circumstance. The taxicab incident was the last straw and helped me snap out of my newly accepted passivity due to battle fatigue. As I sat there in the airport and cried, I realized I had been playing the role of a victim. I had to remind myself that I was victorious in God and His plans were bigger than what I could see in the natural. Then God reminded me that the battle wasn't mine, but it belonged to Him. I'm happy to say that God always wins. It was God's plan all along to use the trials and tribulations to accelerate my journey to fulfill a bigger purpose than I had even imagined.

Focus on what God is doing in the spirit realm.

Often we miss the God opportunities because we are focused on the immediate trials and challenges instead of on the bigger picture. King Joash is a great example of a person who missed a God opportunity by focusing on the natural realm rather than the spirit realm. He was so focused on the impending death of the prophet Elisha that he couldn't see that God was positioning him for an unstoppable victory.

In 2 Kings 13 the prophet Elisha was sick and near death. King Joash went to him and wept because the prophet was dying. While Joash was there, Elisha told him to take a bow and arrow and shoot it. Joash did as instructed, and Elisha declared, "The arrow of the deliverance of the LORD, and the arrow of deliverance from Aram; for you must strike Aram in Aphek until you have destroyed them" (v. 17, MEV).

Then Elisha told King Joash to "take the arrows" and "strike the ground." "So he struck it three times and stood there. Then the man of God was angry with him and said, 'You should have struck it five or six times. Then you would have stricken Aram until you had finished them. Now you will strike Aram just three times'" (2 Kings 13:18–19, MEV).

Just as Joash didn't discern the spiritual repercussions of a natural test, we too often miss what God is doing. There are times when God will allow dysfunctional or needy people to cross our path because He wants to see how we will respond. Other times God will allow us to go through a time of suffering so He can see whether we will give Him our all—mind, body, and spirit—or be halfhearted in our commitment, as Joash was. God is watching what we do while we wait for His *kairos* to bring our restoration and redemption.

Surround yourself with godly people.

You can tell your future by the company you keep. Proverbs 11:14 says, "Where there is no counsel, the people fall; but in the multitude of counselors there is safety" (MEV). Isolating yourself during a trial is one of the worst things you can do. "Where two or three are gathered," there God will be in their midst (Matt. 18:20). One thing I love about the Majestic Life member who won the city commission seat is she surrounded herself with as many strong leaders as possible. As a result, she was strengthened to stand through the attacks.

Never forget you are a spiritual being in an earthly realm. You are in this world, but you are not of this world. Our focus should never be on our circumstance but on our God, for we walk by faith and not by sight. You may feel as though you are in a dead-end job, your ministry is in the midst of famine and there's no rain in sight, or you're past your prime and too old to begin something new. Focus on what God is doing in the spirit realm, and view each trial and tribulation as an opportunity for forward movement and promotion. And by all means, surround yourself with those who want what God desires for you to have. God will redeem the time that has been lost, and He will accelerate your progress toward your purpose and destiny.

Chapter 3

THE TAPESTRY OF LIFE

———————— ❦ ————————

WHEN I THINK of the way God brings together all the puzzle pieces in our lives to form a magnificent picture according to His master plan, I am reminded of a poem often quoted by *The Hiding Place* author Corrie ten Boom. It says:

> My life is but a weaving
> Between my God and me.
> I cannot choose the colors
> He weaveth steadily.
>
> Oft' times He weaveth sorrow;
> And I in foolish pride
> Forget He sees the upper
> And I the underside.
>
> Not 'til the loom is silent
> And the shuttles cease to fly
> Will God unroll the canvas
> And reveal the reason why.

The dark threads are as needful
In the weaver's skillful hand
As the threads of gold and silver
In the pattern He has planned

He knows, He loves, He cares;
Nothing this truth can dim.
He gives the very best to those
Who leave the choice to Him.[1]

—AUTHOR UNKNOWN

The lines of this poem paint a beautiful picture of God's work in our lives. In life, especially during hard times, often all we see are the knotted ends and overlapping threads on the underside of the tapestry. We see the chaos of our busy schedules, the ugly consequences of bad choices, the mess left after a divorce, or the confusion created by an unexpected diagnosis. We don't see the masterpiece God is weaving together on the top side of the tapestry. We don't see how He's giving our pain and problems a purpose and equipping us to fulfill His plan because that part of the picture remains out of view.

The seven years of trials and tribulations I experienced left me bewildered. I didn't understand what was happening to my family and me. I wondered how God was going to salvage our hope and purpose after all the pain and tragedies we had endured. As the poem says, "Oft' times He weaveth sorrow; / And I in foolish pride / Forget He sees the upper / And I the underside."

I thought only of the frayed underside of my tapestry, not fully realizing that God was weaving everything together to create something beautiful in my life. He was turning my chaos into order, and what was meant for my destruction

God was faithfully working out for my good. I just couldn't see it.

It is like a seed planted beneath the surface of the ground. Buried in the darkness of the dirt, a seed eventually will turn into a nourishing plant under the right conditions. But the naked eye cannot see what is being produced. Similarly a mother cannot see the baby in her womb without an ultrasound. She doesn't know if she's having a boy or girl, what the child looks like, or how big he or she is. But even though she can't see what's happening inside her womb, that child is still growing and taking form.

Even when we can't see enough to explain why we are facing that pain, hardship, or trial, we can trust that God sees the full picture, and He will weave every piece together for His glory. "The dark threads are as needful / In the weaver's skillful hand / As the threads of gold and silver / In the pattern He has planned."

In the Book of Genesis, Isaac's wife, Rebekah, had been barren, and the Lord miraculously opened her womb and gave her twins. As the children grew, she felt them struggling within her, but she didn't know why. She inquired of the Lord, and He told her, "Two nations are in your womb, and two peoples from within you shall be divided; the one shall be stronger than the other, the older shall serve the younger" (Gen. 25:23, ESV). Rebekah could not see what was going on within her, so she didn't understand why the manifestation of her promise was causing her so much pain. But when she inquired of the Lord, He told her it was because of what was being birthed inside her.

God is infinite in His wisdom. It was not my desire to pastor again. But when God began to speak to me, He gave me glimpses of what He wanted to do in my life. He revealed

His assignment to me in bits and pieces, giving me just enough information for me to take baby steps toward the promise until the seed He planted in me began to manifest.

During those dark periods in my life I didn't always recognize the power and potential God had placed in me. I couldn't see the masterpiece He was creating, and I wasn't the only one. I heard through the grapevine that people I respected said I would never be able to pastor a large ministry. Obviously they were focusing on the visible, chaotic threads of my life and couldn't discern what God was doing on the topside of my tapestry.

I couldn't focus on what they thought. I had to focus on what God had spoken to me. I did as He instructed, and the ministry grew by the Spirit of the Lord, not by my charisma. Today I am a single woman leading a large church. Nobody but God could have done that. He still chooses the foolish things to confound the wise.

You may not be able to imagine it right now, but I declare that the seed God has placed in you is great! If you feel some discomfort as it grows, that's just an indication of the magnitude of what God is doing in your life. You are God's child, and the plans He has for you are wonderful.

In the Word of God there are many examples of people whose lives looked chaotic and puzzling from the underside. You'll find knots and exposed threads, even though the topside looked like a beautiful masterpiece. Who would have thought that Mary, an unassuming young girl, would birth the Messiah? Who would have expected David, the ruddy redhead who tended sheep, to become the greatest king of Israel? Who would have imagined that Esther, an orphan being raised by her cousin, would be given the responsibility of saving her nation? Your life may be similar. You may not stand out in the crowd. Your life may even seem dysfunctional. But even if others don't see what's inside you, God will bring forth His plans for your life.

It is easy for us to see Jesus's death, burial, and resurrection throughout the text of the New Testament, but prophecies about Jesus's coming are hidden throughout the Old Testament. They were concealed until it was time for them to be revealed. Galatians 4:4 says, "When the fulness of the time was come, God sent forth his Son." Right now our lives may look opposite to what the fullness of time will reveal. We may be entirely unaware of the beauty and the power of what God is working in our lives because all we see are the problems and challenges. But remember, the bigger the baby, the more pain in the birthing experience.

Even though we know in part and prophesy in part, God doesn't want you to stay in the dark about your power and potential. God may not reveal everything He is doing all at once. But He desires for you to recognize your greatness as His child. You "are a chosen generation, a royal priesthood, an holy nation, a peculiar people; that ye should shew forth the praises of him who hath called you out of darkness into his marvellous light" (1 Pet. 2:9).

When we are looking at the underside of the tapestry of our lives, with all its knots and disorder, it's easy to think our world is in disarray. But God is in control, and we belong to Him. He is the One who created us, and we have His divine DNA. He is our source, and He knows exactly what He's doing in our lives, even when we don't.

So please do not complain about the many hats God has given you to wear and what a mess your life looks like from the underside. God is using every strand, every role and responsibility you have, to make you into an individual who can carry the weight of His glory! The designer knows that what we see as disorder on the underside of our tapestry is necessary to produce the ideal result. God sees the order in what we perceive as chaos.

MAKE YOUR WAY TO JESUS

What God sees when He looks at us is nothing like what we see on the underside of our tapestry. But as we run to Him and spend time in His presence, our lives will begin to reflect His masterpiece. This is beautifully illustrated in the story of the woman with the alabaster box. We read in the Gospel of Luke:

> When one of the Pharisees invited Jesus to have dinner with him, he went to the Pharisee's house and reclined at the table. A woman in that town who lived a sinful life learned that Jesus was eating at the Pharisee's house, so she came there with an alabaster jar [or alabaster box] of perfume. As she stood behind him at his feet weeping, she began to wet his feet with her tears. Then she wiped them with her hair, kissed them and poured perfume on them.
> —LUKE 7:36–38, NIV

Before we examine the woman with the alabaster box, I want to draw your attention to where this took place. The Bible tells us Jesus was dining in the home of a Pharisee. Yes, you read that right. What was Jesus doing in the home of a Pharisee? Jesus and the Pharisees did not get along. In Matthew 23 Jesus called the Pharisees hypocrites and said they were full of extortion and greed. He called them a generation of vipers and wondered how they were going to escape hell. The Pharisees were so stuck on the traditions of the law that they couldn't receive the grace and truth Jesus brought. So why was Jesus breaking bread with a Pharisee?

The answer is really so simple and yet so profound. Jesus was dining with Simon the Pharisee because Simon invited Him. I want you to let that sink in for a minute. No matter what your life looks like, no matter how damaged or dysfunctional it seems to you, if you invite Jesus into your situation, He will come. You may have experienced betrayal, divorce, infidelity, sexual perversion, incurable disease, or financial loss. It doesn't matter. Jesus doesn't care about the mess. He wants to be invited into your situation just as it is.

If you try to wait until you get cleaned up before reaching out to Jesus, you will be waiting a long time. Only He can heal and restore. Jesus said, "Here I am! I stand at the door and knock. If anyone hears my voice and opens the door, I will come in and eat with that person, and they with me" (Rev. 3:20, NIV), and "Come to me, all you who are weary and burdened, and I will give you rest" (Matt. 11:28, NIV). Never be afraid of Jesus. Invite Him in. He is at the door knocking, wanting to be part of every situation you face.

Simon the Pharisee invited Jesus to his house, but the woman with the alabaster box was not on the guest list. As a Pharisee, Simon wouldn't have wanted to be anywhere near a woman with a reputation like hers. By all accounts this woman was a well-known prostitute in her city. And that's probably all most people saw when they looked at her— the underside of her tapestry, full of frayed edges and dark threads riddled with knots.

But at some point this woman encountered Jesus. And when she did, everything changed. She saw she was more than her past, more than her problems, more than the things she had done. She glimpsed something beautiful beyond the shame. She saw worth where there had been worthlessness, hope where there had been hopelessness, purpose where there had been nothing but empty space. In that encounter with Jesus, however long or short it may have been, she began to see she was more than just loose threads.

This, I believe, is where her story picks up in Luke's Gospel. We don't know when this woman first met Jesus, but we know she was anxious to find Him again. When she learned where Jesus was going to be, she sought Him out. Let's look again at Luke 7:

> A woman in that town who lived a sinful life learned that Jesus was eating at the Pharisee's house, so she came there with an alabaster jar of perfume. As she stood behind him at his feet weeping, she began to wet his feet with her tears. Then she wiped them with her hair, kissed them and poured perfume on them.
>
> —LUKE 7:37–38, NIV

As someone who had lived a sinful life, she probably was ostracized, talked about, and considered too dirty to be respected by her community. But I believe her encounter with Jesus left her so changed that she became more concerned about getting to Jesus than what people would think. She was like the psalmist who said, "As the deer pants for streams of water, so my soul pants for you, my God. My soul thirsts for God, for the living God. When can I go and meet with God?" (Ps. 42:1–2, NIV). This woman was so desperate for Jesus, she wouldn't let anything stop her from getting to Him—not the customs of that day or those who had judged her for so long.

When she came to Jesus, this woman brought an alabaster

box of precious ointment; in other words, she brought her own worship. She didn't ask to borrow anyone else's alabaster box; she didn't need a praise and worship team, a title, or a position. All she needed was to think about how Jesus set her free. And that made her want to pour her precious perfume onto Jesus.

> When the Pharisee who had invited him saw this, he said to himself, "If this man were a prophet, he would know who is touching him and what kind of woman she is—that she is a sinner."
>
> Jesus answered him, "Simon, I have something to tell you."
>
> "Tell me, teacher," he said.
>
> "Two people owed money to a certain money-lender. One owed him five hundred denarii, and the other fifty. Neither of them had the money to pay him back, so he forgave the debts of both. Now which of them will love him more?"
>
> Simon replied, "I suppose the one who had the bigger debt forgiven."
>
> "You have judged correctly," Jesus said.
>
> Then he turned toward the woman and said to Simon, "Do you see this woman? I came into your house. You did not give me any water for my feet, but she wet my feet with her tears and wiped them with her hair. You did not give me a kiss, but this woman, from the time I entered, has not stopped kissing my feet. You did not put oil on my head, but she has poured perfume on my feet. Therefore, I tell you, her many sins have been forgiven—as her great love has shown. But whoever has been forgiven little loves little."

Then Jesus said to her, "Your sins are forgiven."
—LUKE 7:39–48, NIV

Whenever I read this passage of Scripture, I want to shout! In these words I see how much God loves each of us. The underside of the tapestry of your life may be in disarray. You may have done things you are not proud of. You may feel as though you are not worthy of anything good. But Jesus desires to affirm you and bring you healing. All you have to do is make your way to Jesus.

When Simon the Pharisee was judging the woman in his heart, Jesus heard him and asked Simon a question: If two people owed a moneylender and their debt was canceled, who would love the moneylender more, the one whose debt was great, or the one whose debt was little? Simon said, "The one whose debt was great." And Jesus told him that was correct and explained that the woman loved much because she had been delivered of much.

Our beautiful Savior heard what Simon was thinking and confronted him. You may have enemies unbeknownst to you. Even if they never say a word to you, they may be thinking evil toward you. Jesus knows their hearts, and He will reveal what you need to know. Worshippers don't have to look over their shoulders in paranoia to protect themselves. Jesus knows the hearts of your enemies, and He will protect you.

This woman with the alabaster box was so grateful to Jesus for what He had done for her that she desired to worship Him with everything she had. Simon complained that it was inappropriate for the woman to touch Jesus as she did—to wash His feet with her tears, dry them with her hair, kiss them, and then anoint them with the expensive ointment.

But Jesus validated her manner of worshipping Him and in the process exposed Simon's pride.

When you are a worshipper, you don't have to worry about whether people reject or undermine you. Your worship will expose the enemy's hidden plans. I've seen God do this again and again in my life. My circumstances were extremely unpleasant. I had layers and layers of issues I had to deal with. Many people thought I would never recover. *But God.*

When you're a worshipper, Jesus will protect you from the wicked and the religious. He will exalt you. So don't be a man-pleaser; be a God-pleaser. Give God your all, as this woman did. Worship Him in Spirit and in truth. Jesus will stand for you and validate you. As Exodus 14:14 says, "The Lord shall fight for you, while you hold your peace" (MEV).

The underside of this woman's tapestry was unattractive. It was so repulsive, people mocked her. But this woman with a once-messed-up life poured precious ointment on Jesus, and as she was anointing Jesus, she was receiving the same anointing. What she poured on Jesus also got on her. The same fragrance she rubbed on Jesus rubbed off on her. When you worship Jesus, you become more like Jesus. You begin to look and sound more like Jesus, and you walk in the same power in which Jesus walked.

As the fragrance of the ointment filled the room, the woman's tapestry became more beautiful than those of the highest religious leaders of her day and more beautiful than those of even some of Jesus's disciples. The underside of her tapestry looked nothing like the way Jesus saw her or the way others soon would see her.

The underside of her tapestry wasn't appealing, but Jesus made her beautiful. Looking at me from the outside, it seemed unlikely that I would be chosen to be a lead pastor and community leader. I don't fit the mold of a large-church pastor. I am mild-mannered, a little bit country, and a lot feminine. But God wasn't looking at my external qualifications. "The sacrifices of God are a broken spirit: a broken and a contrite heart, O God, thou wilt not despise" (Ps. 51:17). God does not look at your outward appearance. He is searching your heart.

TRAIN YOUR HANDS FOR WAR

Greatness is in you, and God is working all the events of your life together to bring about His master plan, but that doesn't mean you won't have to fight to see it manifest. First Timothy 6:12 tells us, "Fight the good fight of faith," and Jude 3 tells us to "earnestly contend for the faith." The fight was bestowed upon us in Genesis 3:15 when God said, "And I will put enmity between thee and the woman, and between thy seed and her seed; it shall bruise thy head, and thou shalt bruise his heel." Enmity is "a feeling or condition of hostility; hatred; ill will" toward someone or something.[2] The enmity we have toward the enemy is innate, but that doesn't mean we innately know how to fight him.

A boot camp is an intensive training program often used to improve one's physical fitness or skills in a particular subject area. Military personnel always go through boot camp right after entering the service. Boot camp is intended to break you down and then build you back up in a more disciplined, fit form so you will be prepared for battle.

Spiritual boot camp is much the same. A good spiritual fighter must be trained. David said in Psalm 144:1, "Praise be to the LORD my Rock, who trains my hands for war, my fingers for battle" (NIV). In order for us to be effective in our spiritual walk and to harness the enmity God gave us to successfully wage war against the enemy, we must go through a spiritual conditioning. Without that training, you may find yourself fighting in your flesh by being catty, vindictive, or emotional. Without going through spiritual conditioning, your blows will be misdirected.

Going to church regularly and reading the Word aren't enough in themselves to get you properly conditioned for spiritual warfare. Those things alone won't make you a mature spiritual soldier. You must let that Word get into your heart and influence your actions so you behave more like Jesus. You must yield to the Holy Spirit's leading and allow Him to fill you up until you exude His character. (See Galatians 5:22–23.) And you must walk in love, as Jesus instructed: "A new command I give you: Love one another. As I have loved you, so you must love one another. By this everyone will know that you are my disciples, if you love one another" (John 13:34–35, NIV).

As 1 Corinthians 13 states, love is patient and kind; it doesn't envy or brag; it isn't rude or selfish, nor is it easily provoked. Godly love doesn't rejoice in others' misfortune— even those who have done us wrong—but it rejoices in the truth. The enemy hates the truth; he is the father of lies, and the truth is not in him (John 8:44). When you have been spiritually conditioned, you will be able to stand for the truth in love and pray for your enemies, and in so doing you will overcome the evil one.

That's the kind of maturity Pastors Joel and Ylawnda Peebles of City of Praise Family Ministries in Landover, Maryland, needed when they were faced with an unexpected spiritual and legal battle. Pastor Joel's mother founded City of Praise, and after she died, he was kicked off the board and out of the church. The board then hired a new pastor.

However, many of the members left the church with Pastor Joel, and they gathered together for worship in local high school auditoriums. It took three years of fighting on his knees and through the courts, but Pastor Joel was reinstated as pastor after a judge invalidated the church board's actions against him.[3]

I was so proud of Pastors Joel and Ylawnda for walking in the grace of God for three long years. It must have been devastating for Pastor Joel to see the work his parents built from nothing taken away by a church board. And all this was happening at a time when he was grieving his mother's death. They could have spoken ill of people or taken their complaints to the media. But they did their due diligence in prayer and in the courts. I was shocked when some people suggested they should have walked away and started over. I don't think God would have gotten any glory from that because I believe the vision God gave that ministry had yet to be completed. So the Lord taught them how to fight in the spirit and not the flesh, and they prevailed.

The battle Pastors Joel and Ylawnda fought was public, but sometimes the battles we fight are not plain for all to see. Before the woman could freely break the alabaster box for Jesus, she had to break out of the box in which society placed her. In those days, women were not always allowed to fellowship with men at gatherings, so she had to overcome successfully the barriers and limitations that were set before her to get to Jesus. Breaking out of the box the enemy, your flesh, or fear has placed you in can be overwhelming. That's because the box is designed to smother you to keep you from God's will. Refuse to let anything keep you from walking in what God has put inside you.

It would have been easier for Pastors Joel and Ylawnda

just to stay in the box of "give up." That's what many people expected of them. But instead they stirred up their faith, broke out of the box, and warred in the spirit until God gave them the victory.

BREAK UP WITH YOUR PAST

Once the woman with the alabaster box pressed past the barriers around her to give Jesus her worship, she had to go a step further. She also had to break up with her past. That's the only way she could move forward into the future God had for her.

The songwriter was right. Breaking up is hard to do, even when you're convinced it's necessary. It's not easy to break free from the past. Just consider the Israelites after they were delivered from slavery in Egypt.

> Is not this the word that we did tell thee in Egypt, saying, Let us alone, that we may serve the Egyptians? For it had been better for us to serve the Egyptians, than that we should die in the wilderness.
>
> And Moses said unto the people, Fear ye not, stand still, and see the salvation of the LORD, which he will shew to you to day: for the Egyptians whom ye have seen to day, ye shall see them again no more for ever. The LORD shall fight for you, and ye shall hold your peace.
> —EXODUS 14:12–14

The Israelites thought the devil they knew was better than the unknown dangers of the wilderness. The woman with the alabaster box could have chosen to believe the same way—don't rock the boat; leave things as they are. But instead she chose to believe that she did not have to live with shame forever. So she pressed her way to Jesus and let Him change the way she saw her past, present, and future.

In the Book of Hosea the Word of God speaks of breaking up fallow ground: "Break up your fallow ground: for it is time to seek the LORD, till he come and rain righteousness upon you" (Hosea 10:12). Merriam-Webster's dictionary defines *fallow* as "cultivated land that is allowed to lie idle during the growing season."[4] The ground being referred to in Hosea 10 was land that once gave forth a harvest but had become barren and produced only weeds and thorns. Therefore the person cultivating the land would have to "break up" the fallow ground, meaning he had to clear it of weeds and debris before seed could be sown.[5]

Hosea could identify with the need to break up the fallow ground. He remembered Israel at the peak of her victory and success. He remembered how God performed miracles for His people, fought their battles, gave them land, and put their enemies to an open shame. But now that the Israelites had sinned against their loving God, they were no longer bearing the fruit of victory. Hosea was admonishing the Israelites to stop trying to plant their spiritual seed in hard ground filled with thorns and weeds, but to break up the ground so the soil would be conducive for God to move mightily in their midst again.

You must break up the fallow ground in your life so the seed God has planted in you can bear fruit. If you don't, you could become stagnant. As Matthew's Gospel says, if we don't break up fallow ground, thorns will come and choke out the harvest: "He also that received seed among the thorns is he that heareth the word; and the care of this world, and the deceitfulness of riches, choke the word, and he becometh unfruitful" (Matt. 13:22).

God requires us to have clean hands and a pure heart, no matter what we've gone through. You may want to justify why you no longer trust anyone, or why you have become hardened and cold toward people. You may think you have a right to be distant from God and even are justified in your bitterness because you were betrayed and abused in the past. You must not become cold, unfruitful, and fallow. A heart has to be tender to produce a harvest.

John 12:24 says, "Verily, verily, I say unto you, Except a corn of wheat fall into the ground and die, it abideth alone: but if it die, it bringeth forth much fruit." Dying to self isn't easy, but self-sacrifice yields a great anointing. During my seven-year period of trials I had become disappointed in church people. But I didn't want my heart to become hard and make me unfruitful. So I constantly reminded myself that those who hurt me are people and not God.

We all make dumb mistakes. Don't allow yourself to become disillusioned and shut people out. Hebrews 12:14–15 tells us, "Follow peace with all men, and holiness, without which no man shall see the Lord: Looking diligently lest any man fail of the grace of God; lest any root of bitterness springing up trouble you, and thereby many be defiled." If we let them spring up, bitterness and jealousy will take root and choke out our blessings and peace.

The Lord will strengthen you to break up the fallow ground in your life, but He won't do it for you. Scripture tells us that God gives us the "power to get wealth" (Deut. 8:18). Every harvest God gives us—whether it's financial, spiritual, emotional, or physical—requires us to go get it. Do you think farmers get upset when their fields are overflowing with produce and the tree branches are about to break because they have so much fruit? No! They are thrilled. And guess what?

They go get it! For some reason, in the body of Christ, many wait for God to lay their harvest in their lap. They don't ever want to plant a seed, till the land, or harvest the fields.

Don't let that be true of you. The tapestry God is weaving in your life is beautiful. The seed He has planted in you is great. Break up the fallow ground in your life, and go get your harvest.

Chapter 4

EMBRACING THE
DREADED PUZZLE PIECES

THROUGH ALL THE twists and turns in my life, the picture on my box—God's plan for me—never changed. But the path to my destination included a trip to the back side of the desert, where God allowed me to experience the wilderness. God did this many times in Scripture. Abraham, Jonah, David, Moses, Joseph, Elijah, Jesus, and so many others experienced what I call the back side of the desert as part of their journey to fulfill God's call on their lives. It is a place of loneliness, barrenness, and weariness, where God often feels far away. But God isn't actually far from us; He uses these times in the wilderness to draw us closer to Him and strengthen our faith.

After his conversion the apostle Paul disappeared for three years into the desert. There he allowed the Holy Spirit to teach him the ways of God and shape him according to the Father's will. The Lord continued to work on Paul after he left the desert. But it was his desert experience that ignited Paul's passion for Jesus and prepared him for ministry.

Everyone who has read his letters has witnessed the work God performed in his heart when he was in the desert.[1]

Don't be surprised if you have to spend time on the back side of the desert. No one desires this puzzle piece, but don't let it strike fear in your heart. It's on the back side of the desert, when life is wearisome and even painful, that God shows you how to give birth to your purpose. It is there that He strengthens you for the massive assignment He has given you.

My discombobulated seven-year journey was my experience on the back side of the desert. Though the storms were raging all around me, God protected me in His massive arms and cared for me with His sweet, tender love. Then He gave me the grace to emerge with a greater anointing. I can look back on those seven years and see how that experience helped me develop a deeper faith and trust in God. I've learned that God uses even those dreaded puzzle pieces as part of His plan.

I am the proud mother of four children, two in their early twenties and two in their late teens. My oldest son, Zachery Tims III, was diagnosed with severe cerebral palsy at birth. This is a puzzle piece that any parent initially would dread. I became pregnant during the second month of my marriage, but that's not the kicker. I got pregnant again just two months after my first baby was born. When I had been married less than two years, I had two babies who were eleven months apart. Yikes!

Finding out your child has special needs can be quite intimidating, especially when you're only twenty-five years old. When we received the news of Zachery's diagnosis, it was frightening. We had no idea how we would handle this puzzle piece God put in our lives.

Through the years Zachery has had multiple surgeries and countless therapies. As a young mother I spent hours praying over my son. I took him to a series of specialists and many healing services. Yet I watched as other children Zachery's age began sitting up, crawling, and walking while my son could do none of those things.

Fast-forward more than twenty years, and though I once dreaded the challenges of having a child with special needs, I am now amazed as I watch my beautiful son. I love him with all my heart and have learned so much about joy and perseverance from his example. He currently is wheelchair-bound and has been labeled nonverbal, but those closest to him understand him quite well. Zachery can use his left hand at about 60 percent capacity and his right hand at about 20 percent, so it is very difficult for him to complete many everyday tasks. But he goes to both services each Sunday and then to Wednesday evening service.

He has a standing wheelchair that allows him to be upright during services, and Zachery uses it to stand up and give God praise during praise and worship. Zachery's almost baritone voice resounds above those around him. He doesn't sing on key, and he isn't clearly understood, but Zachery's praise is beautiful and anointed because it comes from a pure heart. He also serves in our honor guard (ushers) department. I can't help but smile when I see him around the church. Zachery has more challenges than most people, but he doesn't let any of them stop him. He easily could make up excuses as to why he is unable to attend services or have a bad disposition, but He presses forward. I am so proud to be Zachery's mother. God is birthing greatness in him, and I believe one day his testimony will be even more awesome than it already is. Though this puzzle piece is still challenging and difficult, I've gained so much from it.

I felt it necessary to talk about Zachery because rarely do people view those with special needs as individuals with dreams and desires. Instead they'd rather hide or ignore people with special needs. Zachery desires to go to college, get a job, get married, have children, and become a preacher. Most of the medical community would say those are unattainable goals. Yet we are standing in faith for the manifestation of Zachery's healing. It breaks my heart as a mother to know that Zachery wants to date, just like any other young man, but has had a difficult time meeting someone compatible. His puzzle pieces look nothing like what I had envisioned for him.

Zachery is trapped in a body that does not permit him to walk or speak clearly. He is hindered by his own body. Did God cause Zachery to have cerebral palsy? I say no, but He did allow it, because nothing happens in the earth realm without God's allowing it. He saw fit to include this difficult piece in Zachery's puzzle as well as in mine, so we are choosing to trust God for Zachery's complete healing.

Some puzzle pieces are extremely trying. Perhaps you can relate. If you are experiencing the back side of the desert through an illness, a broken relationship, a financial collapse, the loss of a loved one, or a struggling business, take heart. You've probably heard successful people talk about going through some sort of desert experience that brought them to a crossroads. When asked whether they would change anything about their journey, they usually reply, "No. Everything I've gone through brought me to my place of success." They've come to appreciate the puzzle pieces they once dreaded.

Joseph had to spend many years on the back side of the desert. It was this experience that led him from the pit to the palace and to become second in command in all of Egypt. In Genesis 50:20 Joseph told his brothers, "But as for you, ye thought evil against me; but God meant it unto good, to bring to pass, as it is this day, to save much people alive." Joseph could see how all the things he experienced on the back side of the desert got him where he was that day. God sometimes allows things we dread into our picture, but He will use them to build our spiritual stamina and deepen our confidence in Him.

Lealzo Howard, whom we affectionately call Lebo, stands hefty at six feet five inches and is assistant director of our security department at Majestic Life. At one time it was common to see him walking slowly across the campus with wires hanging from his shirt. Lebo's dreaded puzzle piece was his need for a heart and kidney transplant. Year after year Lebo believed God for either a creative miracle or a transplant. Lebo maintained positive conversation and even decided to host 6:00 a.m. prayer every Friday at church. His hunger for God grew as he remained steadfast in prayer.

Finally Lebo was placed on the organ transplant list. He expected at least a six-month wait, but Lebo received a new heart and kidney in a matter of days. Lebo's once-dreaded puzzle piece is now his testimony!

Caring for Zachery is difficult and labor-intensive, especially as a single woman, but my love for him is greater than the hardship his care presents. This puzzle piece has shown me how God can love me with all my imperfections because that is how I love Zachery. It also has allowed me to understand that my heavenly Father is always there for me, as I am always there for Zachery. My experience with Zachery draws me closer to God and causes me to fall more and more in love with Him.

MORE THAN A CONQUEROR

Don't think God doesn't love you because He allowed a dreaded puzzle piece in your life. Even in the midst of the desert and in the face of detours and wilderness experiences, God loves us extravagantly. The Bible says in Romans 8:35, "Who shall separate us from the love of Christ? shall tribulation, or distress, or persecution, or famine, or nakedness, or peril, or sword?" This verse lets us know we may experience difficult times, but that does not mean God has forgotten us.

Paul says *nothing* can separate us from God's love, and then he gives us a list of dreaded puzzle pieces: tribulation, distress, persecution, famine, nakedness, peril, and the sword. These terms are not commonly used today to describe the kinds of problems we face, so I took the liberty of giving their definitions from Merriam-Webster's dictionary.[2]

- Tribulation—"distress or suffering resulting from oppression or persecution; a trying experience"

- Distress—"pain or suffering affecting the body, a bodily part, or the mind; a painful situation; a state of danger or desperate need"

- Persecution—the state of being harassed or punished "in a manner designed to injure, grieve, or afflict, specifically to cause to suffer because of belief"

- Famine—"an extreme scarcity of food; a great shortage"

- Nakedness—the state of being "devoid of customary or natural covering"

- Peril—"exposure to the risk of being injured, destroyed, or lost"

- Sword—"an agency or instrument of destruction"

I am sure you have had at least one of these awful puzzle pieces in your past or present.

When Paul asks, "Who shall separate us from the love of Christ?," he doesn't answer the question right away; instead he quotes Psalm 44:22 in the next verse: "As it is written, For thy sake we are killed all the day long; we are accounted as sheep for the slaughter" (Rom. 8:36). This seems a little odd. Why did Paul quote that Old Testament scripture at that particular moment?

In the Book of Romans, Paul was speaking to the new converts in Rome. Christians were not welcome there and were going through much persecution. The statement "We are like sheep slaughtered" spoke to the fact that Christians were constantly being persecuted, even though they were not aggressive. They were persecuted simply because they chose to follow Christ. In Romans 8:35 Paul was letting the new believers know that as Christians they would experience tribulation; being saved wouldn't keep them from suffering.

Yet Paul also gives them hope in the next several verses:

> No, in all these things we are more than conquerors through him who loved us. For I am convinced that neither death nor life, neither angels nor demons, neither the present nor the future, nor any powers, neither height nor depth, nor anything else in all

creation, will be able to separate us from the love of
God that is in Christ Jesus our Lord.
—ROMANS 8:37–39, NIV

Did you catch that? Paul's answer to "Will difficult circumstances separate us from the love of Christ?" was, "No."

Paul then lets us know that in the midst of trials and suffering God made us to be more than conquerors. To conquer
means to gain control of or subdue by force. So what does
it mean to be *more than* a conqueror? You may have heard
being more than a conqueror defined as having already won
the battle before the fight begins or having God fight the
battle for you. Those explanations are true, but I'd like to
give you something else to consider. Romans 8:37 says, "No,
in all these things we are more than conquerors" (NIV). The
operative word is *in*. How do we respond when we're *in*
"all these things"? We can choose to respond in a way that
satisfies our flesh, or we can choose to respond in a way
that honors God, advances His kingdom, and thus brings
eternal results.

Nick Vujicic is a popular evangelist who was born with no
legs and no arms. Despite his disability, Nick is crisscrossing
the globe sharing the powerful gospel of Jesus Christ. That's
how he has chosen to respond in the midst of hardship. If
Nick is able to persevere despite the challenges he faces in
life, we have no excuse for not pressing through our trials.

I read a blog recently in which the author explained the
difference between being a conqueror and being more than a
conqueror this way: He said conquerors overcome their enemies by confrontation or force; they use fear to get them to
submit, and their victory is temporary because it lasts only
as long as the "conqueror" has the upper hand. Those who

are more than conquerors transform lives and circumstances to God's glory through suffering and love; they convert enemies into friends and threats into opportunities, and thus make an eternal impact. In other words, being a conqueror is about the benefit to the conqueror; being more than a conqueror is about the benefit to God's kingdom.[3]

Nick Vujicic and Zachery are defeating the enemy by leading people to Jesus Christ in the midst of their own difficulties. They are not using intimidation and manipulation to convert souls to Christ, as some religions do. Nick and Zachery operate in the power of the love of God, and their dreaded puzzle piece has been a conduit to draw many to Christ. To be more than a conqueror in the midst of tribulation and distress means you are yielding to the Lord so He can use you. And when you do this, your preaching is not in vain, your love bears fruit, and generations are affected by the power of God.

I personally believe that God trusts some to deal with dreaded puzzle pieces to allow His glory and grace to penetrate the hearts of unbelievers. Nick Vujicic gets attention from believers and unbelievers alike because of the way he has responded to the challenges he has faced in life. Zachery's smile, laugh, and caring gestures bless everyone who comes in contact with him. Zachery pursues God. He's at every outreach event. He prays with sincerity and faith, and he worships with passion. In my opinion Zachery is an example of being more than a conqueror. Cerebral palsy, by all accounts, should hinder his joy and walk with God. Instead, Zachery's diagnosis is magnifying God's love to those who feel unlovable and rejected. His dreaded puzzle piece has allowed him to reach some who may never set foot in a church.

Genard McNeil had never experienced an intimate

relationship with the Lord and spent lots of time in the streets doing things he isn't proud of. Genard testifies that when he was at some of his lowest moments, Zachery would call him to check on him and express his love. Zachery has been diagnosed as nonverbal, but Genard was able to understand him and sense the love in Zachery's voice. Zachery's disability actually emphasized his sincerity and the pure love of Christ exuding from his heart. Genard often testifies that Zachery is one of the main reasons he doesn't give up when things are difficult.

When I was handed the puzzle pieces of infidelity, separation, divorce, losing everything, the death of my ex-husband, and the loss of the church I cofounded, I didn't realize God wanted to use them to make me into more than a conqueror. The debilitating grief caused by death and betrayal is almost indescribable. There were many times when I wanted to shout from the rooftops, "I can't bear this!" Or worse, I wanted to take matters into my own hands and not follow the leading of the Holy Spirit. But I chose instead to forgive and allow God's love and grace to fill my heart. This thwarted the enemy's strategy to create discord and a spectacle in the body of Christ, and it allowed me to become an example for Christ who might lead some to trust the Lord. Dreaded puzzle pieces, such as health problems, physical challenges, or financial devastation, can transform your life for the better if you let God use them to refine you.

It's Time to Deliver

Ultimately God wants to use the tests and trials on the back side of the desert to bring you into your destiny. We read in Micah 4:10:

Be in pain, and labour to bring forth, O daughter of
Zion, like a woman in travail: for now shalt thou go
forth out of the city, and thou shalt dwell in the field,
and thou shalt go even to Babylon; there shalt thou
be delivered; there the LORD shall redeem thee from
the hand of thine enemies.

This was spoken while the children of Israel were in captivity. For seventy years they lived in an open field instead of
in homes. Then a ruler named Cyrus took the city of Babylon
and made himself master of the whole empire. When he
took power, Cyrus delivered the Jews from their bondage
and allowed them to return to their own land.[4]

Being on the back side of the desert will force you out of
your comfort zone, out of your place of average. The children
of Israel were not in their comfy homes but in open fields,
exposed to the elements. My comfort zone was being financially stable with my husband's support. When I was pushed
into the open field of having to be the sole provider for my
family, I felt isolated and lost, but God steadily guided me.
I learned to take the Lord at His word, and God proved
Himself strong in my life. When I was out of my comfort
zone, God showed me His unconditional love for me and I
trusted His ability to provide for my every need.

During their time of captivity the Israelites' homes and
possessions had been destroyed, and I'm sure they spent
much time thinking about the good old days. There are
times when you will choose to reminisce about the way
things used to be before you were given your dreaded puzzle
piece. If you're not careful, you can become a prisoner of
your mind. Living in the past or rehearsing past situations
will limit your movement forward. The more you stand in

faith for your future, the sooner you will go into labor to birth your destiny.

Micah 4:10 says, "Be in pain, and labour to bring forth." Pregnancy is a common metaphor used in the Word of God. Here in Micah we see that the Israelites were going through hardship before they gave birth. Your dreaded puzzle piece may last a few years, as it was with Lebo, or it may last many years, as it is with my son Zachery. God promises to be with you no matter how long it takes Him to birth His purpose for bringing that puzzle piece into your life.

During pregnancy a woman's body enlarges and changes to accommodate the growing child. In much the same way, when God is birthing something in you while you're on the back side of the desert, you will undergo changes. You won't look like you did before you entered the back side of the desert. Your countenance and your attitude will change as you grow in God. Your appetite for God will increase, and God will stretch you beyond belief. It's all because He's preparing you for something greater.

I assure you that your season on the back side of the desert will not last forever. God promises to deliver you out of the hand of your enemy, just as He delivered the Israelites out of Babylon when Cyrus took command. It was while they were held captive by their enemy that their hearts became desperate for freedom, and they wanted God's intervention. God was doing to His people what some parents do when they choose to let their young adult child spend a night in jail instead of bailing him out. God was teaching them a lesson.

For you, the back side of the desert can be anywhere that causes introspection, repentance, stretching, and growth. It could be a literal jail cell, a hospital room, a school building, an office, a church, or a luxury home with no love. This dreaded puzzle piece tests your strength or reveals your lack thereof. Whatever the back side of your desert looks like, God uses the pain to help you grow and birth His purpose in your life.

But just as it is in the natural, when God is birthing something in your life, the labor can be extremely painful. In my case, the Holy Spirit became my spiritual epidural. His presence helped relieve some of the harsh pain and gave me strength to endure by His grace. He taught me how to PUSH: pray until something happens. Don't abort the seed of your destiny because of the pain. In the natural, women feel as if they are dying when giving birth. So is it in the spirit. You are not dying; the baby is coming.

Some people make the mistake of using alcohol, drugs, sex, and food to stop the pain they experience during the birthing process. Don't fall into that trap. If you succumb to worldly painkillers, your spiritual baby will be subjected to birth defects, and you will not be as effective in the call God has for you.

Once you have travailed in the spirit and have birthed your promise, you still have work to do. It is imperative that you also push out the placenta. The placenta is an organ located in the uterus, where the baby develops. Pushing out the placenta can be quite painful. But if you allow the placenta to remain, it can cause infections. The placenta carries detailed biological information unique to the baby, including the DNA and blood type. The information in the placenta is the essence of who we are.

There is a placenta in the spiritual birthing process as well; it's called your testimony. Your testimony gives detailed information about what God birthed in you. God wants to use it to change lives and help others birth their purpose. If you keep your testimony to yourself, you and others may think that somehow you obtained the promise without the help of the Holy Spirit. Not acknowledging God's precious Spirit can cause spiritual infections such as pride and arrogance. Revelation 12:11 says, "They overcame him by the blood of the Lamb, and by the word of their testimony." Your testimony will help others increase their faith and keep you ever mindful of God's hand in your life.

DON'T GIVE UP

My dear friend Tanya and her husband, Ron, experienced a horrible blow when Ron was diagnosed with Moyamoya disease. It is a cerebrovascular disorder that has caused him to lose his capacity to walk. As a result of the Moyamoya disease, Ron had five strokes and had to have bypass surgery on both sides of his brain in order to prevent him from stroking out and dying. That means he is unable to dress himself, use the restroom, or interact socially with others as he once did. Ron is an extremely dynamic teacher, and he has a personality that is larger than life. But his body is not allowing him to function as he did before, and because he is the senior pastor of their church, Tanya has had to take on all his duties while maintaining her responsibilities as mother, co-pastor, and itinerate speaker.

Despite Ron's limitations, he presses to the house of God. He remains in great spirits and trusts the Lord regardless of his circumstances. I can only imagine how many doctors and nurses are encouraged by his great faith. His testimony of endurance is helping lead people to Christ.

When you're on the back side of the desert waiting for God to birth His purpose in your life, it's easy to become discouraged. The enemy even may attempt to manipulate people and circumstances to make you quit. If you're not aware of his devices, you'll allow people's negativity to cause you to give up or become vexed.

Both Tanya and I have received negative medical reports regarding our loved ones. It can be difficult when scientific evidence consistently and persistently presents to you reasons to lose hope. But the more we are afflicted, the more God multiplies our spiritual strength. As we commune with God, we are motivated to trust Him, and our impossible situations begin to seem possible through Him.

Whom God has blessed, no man can curse. Please don't let your circumstances determine your destination. You also may have been diagnosed with an incurable illness, or maybe you've been molested, raped, betrayed, or bullied. Or perhaps you were promiscuous, a substance abuser, or rebellious. Your destiny still can be great in God.

In Exodus chapter 1 the enemy tried to thwart the Israelites' destiny by manipulating Pharaoh to put them in bondage. The enemy was intimidated by their numbers and thought enslaving them would slow their growth and make them less of a threat. Yet even under hard circumstances the Hebrews continued to multiply. How? The answer is easy. God was with them. Many of us have experienced—or are experiencing—seriously difficult times. Yet the more the challenges of life try to take you down, the more anointing can be produced in your life, resulting in more blessings, increase, and multiplication. But that will happen only if you let God complete the work He is doing during your desert experience.

Delivering a baby is quite painful, but a woman in labor can't decide in the middle of labor to get up and go home because the pain is too great. She must go through the entire labor and delivery. Unfortunately we see spiritual abortions from folk who refuse to go through difficult seasons.

The Bible says in 1 Peter 4:12–13, "Beloved, think it not strange concerning the fiery trial which is to try you, as though some strange thing happened unto you: But rejoice, inasmuch as ye are partakers of Christ's sufferings; that, when his glory shall be revealed, ye may be glad also with exceeding joy." And we read in John 16:21, "When a woman is giving birth, she has pain, because her hour has come. But as soon as she delivers the child, she no longer remembers the anguish for joy that a child is born into the world" (MEV). Both of these scriptures let us know that we must go through the hardship in order to receive the greater thing God has for us.

GUARD YOUR SEED

The Bible tells us, "Resist the devil, and he will flee" (James 4:7). Resisting is one leg in the battle. If the enemy can't stop you with one trick, he will try another. You must be aware that if the enemy can't stop you, he will go after your seed. In Exodus 1:22 Pharaoh commanded that all Hebrew males be killed at birth because the Hebrew population was outgrowing the number of Egyptians. Your seed represents your future and destiny. It may be an unborn business or a business you just started. It may be a ministry, marriage, or natural children. Whatever it is, it's important that you understand that the enemy might attempt to attack it. The enemy went after the male seed during both the time of Moses's birth and the time of Jesus's birth because he wanted to destroy the potential threat while it was in seed form.

Be on alert at all times because the enemy will look for any opportunity to destroy what God is producing in you—and *he always fights dirty.* But always remember that you have the victory. First John 5:3–5 tells us, "In fact, this is love for God: to keep his commands. And his commands are not burdensome, for everyone born of God overcomes the world. This is the victory that has overcome the world, even our faith. Who is it that overcomes the world? Only the one who believes that Jesus is the Son of God" (NIV).

Pharaoh enlisted midwives to kill the male babies as soon as they were born. Strange as it may sound, some of the threats you must protect your seed against are those you might expect to help and support you during your desert season. I know that is a pretty harsh statement. But anyone who has been betrayed by a church leader, spouse, or close friend knows it's true. Judas betrayed Jesus for thirty pieces of silver (Matt. 26:14–15). People will betray you for a lot less. God is the only One who will never fail you.

This is a very hard concept for many of us to understand. When we trust someone, we think that person will never turn on us for any reason. But there are countless parents who have had to deal with the heartbreaking news that a family member molested their child or that a teacher did something perverse with their student. Others have experienced friends' stealing their ideas and sabotaging their dreams instead of supporting them. Psalm 118:8 says, "It is better to trust in the LORD than to put confidence in man" (MEV). This verse counsels us not to put too much confidence in people, status, or positions.

I learned this the hard way. I was devastated when certain people abandoned me while I was going through the wilderness. But fortunately their actions couldn't stop God from birthing His purpose in His set time. Galatians 4:4 says, "But when the set time had fully come, God sent his Son, born of a woman, born under the law" (NIV). And we read in Genesis 21:2, "For Sarah conceived, and bare Abraham a son in his old age, at the set time of which God had spoken to him." What is this set time? It is God's appointed time, and in my experience it comes when a situation or circumstance seems impossible—because then God gets all the glory!

There are many examples in Scripture of God's doing the impossible in His set time. God delivered the Israelites from four hundred years of slavery in Egypt, He saved them from genocide after raising up an orphan girl named Esther to be queen, He brought forth Jesus from the womb of a virgin, and then He raised Him from the grave. The fruit will not fall before it's time; Malachi 3:11 says, "And I will rebuke the devourer for your sakes, and he shall not destroy the fruits of your ground; neither shall your vine cast her fruit before the time in the field, saith the LORD of hosts."

Often I am asked if I still believe that Zachery will be healed. Of course I do. The Word teaches us always to believe and stand in faith no matter how long the miracle takes or how awful the situation looks. Hebrews 11:13 says, "These all died in faith, not having received the promises, but having seen them afar off, and were persuaded of them, and embraced them, and confessed that they were strangers and pilgrims on the earth." I choose to stand in faith, knowing that God is sovereign, and He will answer in His way at His set time.

And while we shouldn't put our trust in people, the Word of God does say we should come in agreement with others who will stand in faith with us and believe God to turn our impossible situations around. Matthew 18:19 says, "Again I say unto you, That if two of you shall agree on earth as touching any thing that they shall ask, it shall be done for them of my Father which is in heaven."

I mentioned previously that Pharaoh instructed the midwives to kill all the male Hebrew babies. Let's look at that passage of Scripture:

> And the king of Egypt spake to the Hebrew midwives, of which the name of the one was Shiphrah, and the name of the other Puah: And he said, When ye do the office of a midwife to the Hebrew women, and see them upon the stools; if it be a son, then ye shall kill him: but if it be a daughter, then she shall live. But the midwives feared God, and did not as the king of Egypt commanded them, but saved the men children alive.
>
> —Exodus 1:15–17

Shiphrah and Puah were midwives who chose to obey God instead of man. Instead of killing the male children, they saved them.

Shiphrah's and Puah's actions sparked a miraculous series of events. The law of synergy states that the whole is greater than the sum of the parts. In other words, working together increases everyone's effectiveness. I can be great at what I do, but when I connect with others who are great, it causes me to be even better.

We must come in agreement with others who have like faith. The word translated "agree" in Matthew 18:19 comes from the Greek word *symphōnéō*, which is where we get the word *symphony*. When an orchestra warms up, it can sound chaotic, but when the members come into agreement to play, it sounds amazing. This is what happened with the midwives. Think about it. Numbers 1:46 says that when the children of

Israel left Egypt, there were 603,550 men who were over the age of twenty. The only way that would have been possible is if they were born during the time when Shiphrah and Puah were midwives. Scholars believe that Shiphrah and Puah somehow organized a group of midwives to hide the male children after their birth. There had to be agreement in order to accomplish such a task.

We need spiritual midwives to help facilitate our miracle. Matthew 18:20 says, "For where two or three are gathered together in my name, there am I in the midst of them." *Yes!* The power of God shows up when there is agreement. The back side of the desert can be a lonely place, but God will bring people to you who will hold you up in prayer. Ask Him to bring these individuals across your path or to show you the ones He already has placed in your life. God will bring you the right support during your desert season. And when you come out of the wilderness and God brings forth His purpose for your pain, be that support for someone else.

Everyone at our church understands that we speak life and healing over my son Zachery and anyone who is suffering from health problems or other kinds of trials. We all come into agreement to be spiritual midwives. We refuse to accept the world's claims that their situations are hopeless. We choose to trust God's Word. We choose to meditate on Romans 8:28 and believe "that all things work together for good to them that love God, to them who are the called according to his purpose."

I encourage you to stand confidently on this truth. The pain and suffering the enemy hopes will harm you on the back side of the desert God will use for your good.

Chapter 5

DEFINING MOMENTS

————————— ❧ —————————

THE BIBLE OFTEN uses images to help us understand the Christian life. Second Timothy 2:3–5 tells us to "endure hardness, as a good soldier." Ephesians 6:11 instructs us to "put on the whole armour of God." We are called "ambassadors for Christ" in 2 Corinthians 5:20, "lively stones" in 1 Peter 2:5, and "the salt of the earth" in Matthew 5:13, just to name a few.

Many times in Scripture the Christian journey is described as a race. You probably know that every aspect of a race is vitally important—the start, the actual race, and the finish. But did you know that at each of those three points we also face defining moments?

What is a defining moment? One pastor explained it this way: "A defining moment is any time in your life in which a choice that you make or an incident that happens causes something in your life to change. It is something that from that moment on defines some aspect of your life."[1]

With that in mind, let's take a look at Hebrews 12:1 (NIV):

> Therefore, since we are surrounded by such a great
> cloud of witnesses, let us throw off everything that
> hinders and the sin that so easily entangles. And let
> us run with perseverance the race marked out for us.

The Hebrew word translated "race" in this text is *agōn*, which also can mean conflict. It is also the root of our English word *agony*.

For many people, one of the hardest things about running a race is getting started. Just when they need to get moving, unexpected disappointments, betrayals, discouragements, and losses hit and weigh them down. Paul's remedy was straightforward. He said to throw off everything that distracts or entangles you—and start running. He was saying, throw away the disappointment, let go of the discouragement, lay the betrayal aside, and get moving. That's your first defining moment. You can't finish a race if you never start.

After my divorce I had no desire to lead another ministry. I had been so hurt, I barely even wanted to attend church, much less pastor one. But when God spoke to me and said I was to lead a new work, I had to lay all of the hurt and distractions aside so I could obey God and move forward.

Choosing to start over in ministry was the hardest decision I had made up to that point. As I stated in chapter 3, I felt inadequate and fragile. I didn't think I had what it would take to be a senior pastor; I thought no one would attend the services and that we wouldn't be able to keep the doors open. But God didn't want me to focus on my flaws and weaknesses; they were distractions. He wanted me to run the race He had set before me. So I made my way to the starting block, got in position, and set off in obedience to God's command.

When I started running the race, God showed Himself

strong. Within two years after starting Majestic Life, we were doing well, even though we had no major financial supporters. God was providing for us. I couldn't take a salary for that entire two-year period, but I was able to use the income from my multilevel marketing business to support my family.

Choosing to start over in ministry was a defining moment for me. Through the process I learned to push past my fears. I found that if I would just step out in obedience, God would be faithful to perform His word. Although it wasn't easy, especially in those first two years, God gave me a peace that I was in His will, and with that confidence I was able to overcome the hurdles that were before me.

During that time my ex-husband was on national television regularly. It seemed as though he was moving full steam ahead, and I was all but forgotten. But that allowed me to keep my focus on the race God put before me. My desire was simply to please the Lord. And if that meant leading a small church in the back parking lot of a strip mall, I was fine with that. Then, just when I was being to breathe a sigh of relief that our ministry had become self-sustained and was picking up momentum, Zachery passed away.

Press Past the Pain

I didn't know how I was going to cope with the grief and raise my children alone. I knew I needed to keep pressing forward, but the pain of Zachery's death was excruciating. This was my next defining moment. I had to decide whether I would keep running the race.

Long-distance runners can experience something called "hitting the wall." They're pushing their bodies so hard, they can exhaust themselves. I've known of people who suddenly became so tired they couldn't get their legs to work, and they just collapsed. That's what it means to hit the wall.

When the pain is persistent and the challenges won't seem to go away, it is easy to lose hope. And living without hope can exhaust you to the point that you think you can't keep going and you're just going to collapse. Sadly, millions of people live this way. They have no hope for tomorrow. Hebrews 11:1 says, "Faith is the substance of things hoped for, the evidence of things not seen." Without hope, faith has nothing to give substance to. That's why Proverbs 13:12 says, "Hope deferred makes the heart sick" (MEV). If we have no hope, our faith will be diminished, and we won't have the stamina to keep running the race.

I often think of the apostle Paul. He ran his race to win, and in the end he was able to say, "I have fought a good fight, I have finished my course, and I have kept the faith" (2 Tim. 4:7, MEV). He gave his all to running the race God set before him.

I want the same to be said of me, but I know from experience that when we feel weighed down by trials, it is hard to keep going. After we learned of Zachery's death, I flew to New York with my mother-in-law, two of New Destiny's leaders, and a member of my church to identify his body. Then the following day we returned to Orlando and went to New Destiny to talk to the members. The church was packed, and New Destiny members were screaming out my name, calling me "Mother," and asking me to return. That was the first of two times I would ever go back to New Destiny. The second time was for Zachery's wake.

It seemed like too much. At that point running the race was excruciatingly difficult. But Hebrews 12:2–3 says, "Looking unto Jesus the author and the finisher of our faith;... consider him that endured such contradiction of sinners against himself, lest ye be wearied and faint in your minds."

When a runner is about to hit the wall, his body is crying out for mercy. But often the toughest battle is in his mind. If he can focus on something bigger than the pain he's in, if he can think about what made him get in the race in the first place, he may be able to find the strength to press forward and finish the race.[2]

The Bible instructs us to look to Jesus so we do not become weary and faint. When I was feeling weary, I had to keep looking to Jesus as my pacesetter. I made it my goal to keep up with Him. When I kept my eyes on Him and followed the pace He set, I had the stamina to press through the grief, to keep pastoring, and to comfort my four children.

When your hope is depleted, the energy to run the race is all but gone. But giving up can't be an option for you.

Again, the apostle Paul wrote:

> Do you not know that in a race all the runners run, but only one gets the prize? Run in such a way as to get the prize. Everyone who competes in the games goes into strict training. They do it to get a crown that will not last, but we do it to get a crown that will last forever. Therefore I do not run like someone running aimlessly; I do not fight like a boxer beating the air. No, I strike a blow to my body and make it my slave so that after I have preached to others, I myself will not be disqualified for the prize.
> —1 Corinthians 9:24–27, niv

Notice that Paul says, "I do not run like someone running aimlessly." Running a race is much different from walking fast. When you run a race, you feel the pain in your body as you push yourself to your limits. Paul instructs us to run this race called life to win. That means it is necessary to give 100 percent. We need to be in it to win it. This is a defining moment. Press beyond the pain.

I used to run track, and I remember our practices being brutal. At times I thought the coach hated us. We would run several miles and then do endurance exercises. It seemed like torture, but our coach was preparing us for the big race. He saw something in us that we couldn't see, and he was pulling the potential out of us. The Word of God shows us in Hebrews that God is a great coach. He disciplines us so we will be strong against the enemy and have a successful spiritual walk. We are encouraged not to complain. And we are reminded that whatever we are going through could never compare to what Jesus endured. We also are reminded that the Lord disciplines those He loves. We must endure the regimen that God gives us because it will make us stronger.

The Bible says:

> "My son, do not make light of the Lord's discipline, and do not lose heart when he rebukes you, because the Lord disciplines the one he loves, and he chastens everyone he accepts as his son." Endure hardship as discipline; God is treating you as his children. For what children are not disciplined by their father? If you are not disciplined—and everyone undergoes discipline—then you are not legitimate, not true sons and daughters at all.
>
> —HEBREWS 12:5–8, NIV

There were times during track practice when the team wanted to take a break. We would look to the coach in desperation, hoping he would hear our groans and have sympathy on us. But usually the coach just would make the practice more intense. God does the same to us when we look to Him to give us a break or take away the pain. We plead our cases to Him, explaining why we don't deserve what we're facing. But God's response is, "Get down and give me fifty more." He says, "Strengthen your feeble arms and weak knees" (Heb. 12:12, NIV). We must not allow ourselves to grow weary during the discipline process.

Recently the body of Christ experienced the shock of several pastors committing suicide over a short period of time.[3] These pastors likely were weary of life's challenges and felt hopeless and as if there was nothing to live for. Galatians 6:9 tells us to "not be weary in well doing: for in due season we shall reap, if we faint not." To be weary means to lose the sense of pleasure, to no longer feel the joy you once felt.

Many things can make you weary—relationships, jobs, ministry, parenting, and even maintaining your health. If you are not careful, your weariness will lead to discouragement. And discouragement leads to quitting. God won't make you move forward; therefore the enemy plays tricks on your mind so you will lose your hope and faith and want to quit.

Let's look again at Galatians 6:9: "Let us not be weary in well doing: for in due season we shall reap, if we faint not." In this verse Paul is telling us we most assuredly will receive the promise we've been waiting for *if* we don't give up. Most people don't catch the revelation in this powerful scripture. It says clearly that you will not reap if you faint. But did you notice why you would faint? Because you exhausted yourself while doing good.

Many people don't reap the promise because they get worn out while waiting on God and give up before they reach the finish line. I understand how easy it is to get exhausted and weary when you've prayed for a prolonged season and there is still no change. But that is not a reason to give up. You must remember that God does not live in our time system. A thousand years is as a day to our Lord. God isn't limited by time. He redeems time. So there's no need to worry when you see others advancing and passing you in the race as long as you're doing God's will. God can change your circumstances in an instant.

To redeem means to buy or purchase something back. This is what Jesus did on the cross. He redeemed us from the curse of the law when He purchased our salvation with His blood. When we talk about God's redeeming the time, we are not talking about His giving us *chronos* time, which refers to seconds, minutes, hours, days, weeks, and months. We are talking about His redeeming *kairos* time.

As I mentioned in chapter 2, *kairos* time is about making those seconds, minutes, hours, days, weeks, and months count. It's about seizing the opportunities God gives us. Ephesians 5:15–17 says, "See then that ye walk circumspectly, not as fools, but as wise, redeeming the time, because the days are evil. Wherefore be ye not unwise, but understanding what the will of the Lord is." God is the author of time, and He can make every struggle, hardship, or delay work in your favor. Ask God to open your eyes to the defining moments in your life; they are all around you.

I had done many national interviews on radio and television after the release of my first book, *When It All Falls Apart*, and they all went well. People were amazed at how I walked with grace and forgiveness throughout the drama. The interviewers were respectful and did not focus on Zachery's infidelities or his death, but on how I stood in love and forgiveness toward those who hurt me. At one point a national magazine contacted me, asking if they could interview me regarding the growth of my church and how I maintained my faith and sanity through the tough times. They assured us they were not going to discuss Zachery's death.

When the article came out, it was completely about Zachery and his death. I couldn't believe they did that. My children were pictured with me in the article. The interviewer came to my home to make sure I felt confident that she would be focusing on my church and my healing process. Yet she manipulated my interview to sell magazines. I was devastated. And I was exhausted.

I had been going through drama for several years already. When was it going to end? Little did I know, God was still reshaping and molding me to prepare me to fulfill His will. Paul wrote in 2 Corinthians 12:7–10:

> And lest I should be exalted above measure through the abundance of the revelations, there was given to me a thorn in the flesh, the messenger of Satan to buffet me, lest I should be exalted above measure. For this thing I besought the Lord thrice, that it might depart from me. And he said unto me, My grace is sufficient for thee: for my strength is made perfect in weakness. Most gladly therefore will I rather glory in my infirmities, that the power of Christ may rest upon me. Therefore I take pleasure in infirmities, in reproaches, in necessities, in persecutions, in distresses for Christ's sake: for when I am weak, then am I strong.

This passage makes it sound like Paul is in a prolonged season of torment. Yet God reminds Paul that His "grace is sufficient," that His "strength is made perfect in weakness."

That is a profound statement. God was letting Paul know that His grace was enough to empower him to endure. God knew what He had put in Paul, and His grace was sufficient to secure the victory. Once Paul got that revelation, he declared that he would rather glory in his infirmities, reproaches, persecutions, and distresses, "that the power of Christ may rest upon [him]."

A Second Wind

When Paul came to the end of himself, that's when God's grace kicked in. In this race called life, we will find ourselves getting weary. We even may feel like we're hitting the wall. Our legs may be in pain, and our chest, tight, but we can't quit. Something remarkable happens when you run until you become weary. You will get a second wind. A second wind is phenomenal because it gives you a burst of energy. Your body feels as if you have just started the race. But the only way to get a second wind is to run until you're exhausted.

After the magazine article incident my ministry team complained to the magazine that the interviewer deceived us and manipulated the article. But our complaints seemed to fall on deaf ears. In the face of what felt like injustice, I decided to keep moving forward. This was another defining moment for me. I was getting closer to the finish line, and the enemy wanted to use the article to distract me from running my race. But I refused to be sidetracked. I chose to throw off the offense that easily could have taken root and keep running the race. That article was not going to keep me from completing my assignment.

Three years after Zachery's death our church found a new building to move into, but securing a loan for the new facility was an uphill battle. After we raised our down payment, a dear bishop friend of ours highly recommended someone to us who potentially could help us secure a good loan. After months of going around in circles with this person and making no progress, we decided to cut ties. Unfortunately we had wasted quite a bit of time working with that individual.

Our ministry decided not to be distracted by this setback but continued to believe that God would make a way for us. Not long after, we secured a loan at a rate we were not too pleased with from a credit union whose covenants were ridiculous. I knew that wasn't God's best; it was another distraction.

Soon after, a local pastor reached out to me after reading a blog my oldest daughter, Zoe, wrote about her journey after her father's death. He was so touched he wanted to know if there was anything we needed. I explained to him our church mortgage situation, and he introduced us to a small bank in Orlando, Florida, from which we were able to secure a loan with a great interest rate. Our mortgage for the new facility, which seats close to two thousand people, is less than what we paid in rent for our facility that sat only five hundred people.

When He miraculously provided a permanent home for our church, God gave me a second wind to run on. God had used me to establish a new work, and we now had a property that we owned. Coming to this moment changed my life forever. I realized that through every scary and uncertain moment in ministry, God had been redefining me. I'm not the same person I was in 1996 when Zachery and I planted New Destiny Christian Center. I am stronger because I have a deeper intimacy with God. I know His grace is sufficient.

God also will give you a second wind as you run your race. The wind of the Spirit will renew your strength and empower you to do things you could not do on your own. It will blow against your back, enabling you to redeem the time that was lost. So how do you let the Holy Spirit renew your strength?

Wait on the Lord.

Isaiah 40:31 says, "They that wait upon the LORD shall renew their strength; they shall mount up with wings as eagles; they shall run, and not *be weary*; and they shall walk, and *not faint*" (emphasis added). If you are ever weary, you must wait on the Lord. I don't mean that you should just sit there looking at your watch; I mean you should wait on Him as a waiter would. Ask the Lord how you can serve Him. Ask Him what He desires. That's when God will renew your strength.

Don't lose hope.

Romans 4:18, 20–21 says, "Who against hope believed in hope, that he might become the father of many nations, according to that which was spoken, So shall thy seed be.... He staggered not at the promise of God through unbelief; but was strong in faith, giving glory to God; and being fully persuaded that, what he had promised, he was able also to perform." God desires for us to maintain our hope. He wants us to be fully convinced that He will do what He promised. This will help us grow strong in faith.

I have had so many defining moments that I can't share them all. But my defining moments led to my redefining moment. God redefined who I am. He made me into another vessel, as Jeremiah 18:4 says: "And the vessel that he made of clay was marred in the hand of the potter: so he made it again another vessel, as seemed good to the potter to make it."

Don't let your circumstances define you. Let God redefine

you through them. What you choose in that defining moment will determine how you finish the race.

Genesis 35:18 tells us that Jacob's wife Rachel died after giving birth. Before she died, she named her son Benoni, which means "son of my sorrow." But Jacob renamed the child Benjamin, which means "son of my right hand." What a huge difference.

God renamed my trial and called it victory. He saw fit to use me to start yet another ministry from what looked like nothing and grow it to over a thousand members in six years. What a miracle! You mustn't listen to the enemy's lies about your ability or God's willingness to bring forth your destiny. God wants to use you for His glory. All you need to do is let Him.

Jesus said, "Flesh gives birth to flesh, but the Spirit gives birth to spirit. You should not be surprised at my saying, 'You must be born again.' The wind blows wherever it pleases. You hear its sound, but you cannot tell where it comes from or where it is going. So it is with everyone born of the Spirit" (John 3:6–8, NIV).

The Spirit of the Lord in this text is likened unto wind that blows wherever it pleases. I live in Central Florida, and we have a hurricane season each year. Sometimes we don't experience inclement weather during hurricane season, and other times we are warned to board up our windows and hunker down because we are in the path of a storm. If we don't board up our windows, the wind might break them and blow glass into the house, causing serious damage.

The wind of the Spirit is the polar opposite. When the wind of the Spirit shows up, we are warned to take the boards down from our eye gates, our ear gates, and our hearts. When you've experienced difficult seasons in your life, it is not uncommon to close yourself off to protect yourself. God says, "Leave everything exposed to the wind of the Spirit." When the wind blows, it will rearrange your spiritual house. It will overturn and uproot. And when the wind has finished blowing, you will be prepared supernaturally for the master's use.

Chapter 6

GOD WILL RESTORE

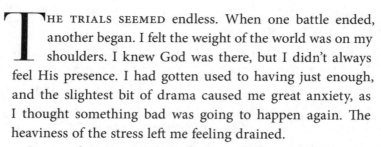

THE TRIALS SEEMED endless. When one battle ended, another began. I felt the weight of the world was on my shoulders. I knew God was there, but I didn't always feel His presence. I had gotten used to having just enough, and the slightest bit of drama caused me great anxiety, as I thought something bad was going to happen again. The heaviness of the stress left me feeling drained.

During this time I did not find comfort or pleasure in the ministry. I had lost everything; I was rebuilding by faith, but on many days I was just going through the motions as an act of obedience. I did everything I needed to do, pressing on by faith, but at times I wondered if things would ever change.

The legal battle to secure my children's inheritance was torturous. And the constant pressure of pastoring, traveling, providing for my family, and being there for my children left me depleted of joy. I started praying that God would send a husband to me. I desperately wanted to be married again and possibly take the role of co-pastor again. *But God!* He wouldn't let it be. God spoke to me clearly, telling me that if I were to marry prematurely, my new husband would possibly get the credit for the success of the ministry. No person was to receive the glory or credit; all the glory belonged to God, similar to what God told Gideon in Judges 7:2: "The LORD said to Gideon, 'You have too many warriors with you. If I let all of you fight the Midianites, the Israelites will boast to me that they saved themselves by their own strength'" (NLT). God wanted me to grow in faith and in His anointing. I was a living testimony of the foolish things confounding the wise.

When I thought I could not bear any more, I realized I didn't have to live this way. I denounced the fear and anxiety, and declared by faith that I would be anxious for nothing "but in every thing by prayer and supplication with thanksgiving" I would let my "requests be made known unto God" (Phil. 4:6–7).

When I chose not to be tormented by fear and anxiety, the Holy Spirit brought comfort. I felt God lift the burden and revive me. I can hardly describe it, but I felt a fresh wind in my spirit. Majestic Life was strengthened too as I walked in a new confidence and anointing. The joy of the Lord became my strength.

In life we all face trying times. Sometimes we feel as if we've lost so much, things will never be the way they once were. It's easy to get discouraged when we've gone through trial after trial; we might even start to think things will never get better. But I want to tell you that God isn't just going to bring you out of the trial; He's going to bring you out better than you were before. God is a restorer. Whether the trial is someone else's fault, your fault, or no one's fault, God will not only bring you out, but He'll also bring you out better than you were before.

In Exodus 22:1 the Bible says, "If a man shall steal an ox, or a sheep, and kill it, or sell it; he shall restore five oxen for an ox, and four sheep for a sheep." And we read in Proverbs 6:30–31: "Men do not despise a thief, if he steal to satisfy his soul when he is hungry; but if he be found, he shall restore sevenfold; he shall give all the substance of his house." Did you notice the pattern? God didn't just restore; He restored with interest.

When God brings us out, we won't be the same. The Hebrew word often translated "restore" is *shuwb*, which means to turn back to God, to refresh, to repair. To restore something means to bring it back to its original state or to an even better condition. It also can mean to take something from the garbage heap and make something special out of it. When a person restores a piece of furniture, he brings it back to its original condition. But when God restores us, He makes us better than we were before.

Before that seven-year season of trials I didn't fully realize all that God had placed in me. I knew I had the ability to minister because I had been doing that for more than fifteen years. But I didn't know God could use me to lead a large church on my own. I didn't know He could use me to start a business and provide financially for my family at the level to which we had grown accustomed. When God brought me out of that seven-year season, I was stronger as an individual and as a leader, more blessed financially, and walking in a greater anointing to do all that He had called me to do.

If you've suffered loss, if you've been through a prolonged season of trials, if you've faced an unexpected illness that has shaken you to the core, don't tell yourself things will never change. Remind yourself that the God you serve is a restorer. I declare to you today that you are not only coming out, but you're also coming out stronger and better than you were before. That should have you shouting amen! God is going to change things in your favor.

You may be wondering why God allowed you to go through the hardship in the first place. Some of the children of Israel questioned why God allowed them to be slaves in Egypt and then to spend years wandering in the wilderness. You may be asking God why you were fired, betrayed, abused, or abandoned. I honestly don't believe that God causes anything bad, but He does allow things to happen to bring about His greater purposes.

We must be forever mindful that there are laws and principles in effect that produce consequences. That's why restoration is a process that begins with repentance.

CUT AWAY THE FLESH

After Moses died and Joshua was chosen to lead the children of Israel, Joshua had all the men circumcised. The generation that had been enslaved in Egypt was now dead, and their children, who had been wandering in the wilderness all their lives, had not been circumcised. God was ready to bring them into their Promised Land, to restore all they had lost and then some, but first the children of Israel needed to cut away their flesh.

In Scripture circumcision represented a type of repentance. Deuteronomy 10:16 says, "Circumcise therefore the foreskin of your heart, and be no more stiffnecked." In this verse removing the filthiness of the flesh from the heart is being likened to removing rebellion. That is why Joshua wanted all the men to be circumcised. It represented the Israelites' repenting of their old way of thinking, letting go of their sin, and submitting themselves fully to God. This is where all restoration begins—in our choosing to cut away our flesh through repentance and become new creatures in Christ (2 Cor. 5:17). When we cut away the flesh, several things happen.

God removes our reproach.

> And after the whole nation had been circumcised, they remained where they were in camp until they were healed. Then the LORD said to Joshua, "Today I have rolled away the reproach of Egypt from you."
> —JOSHUA 5:8–9, NIV

When the Israelites cut away their flesh, the Bible says the reproach on their lives was removed. Reproach is "an expression of rebuke or disapproval" or "a cause or occasion of blame, discredit, or disgrace."[1] Acts 3:19 says, "Repent, then, and turn to God, so that your sins may be wiped out, that times of refreshing may come from the Lord" (NIV). God removes the reproach when you repent. When you repent, your slate is wiped clean, and God is free to restore you.

God tells us in 2 Chronicles 7:14, "If my people, which are called by my name, shall humble themselves, and pray, and seek my face, and turn from their wicked ways; then will I hear from heaven, and will forgive their sin, and will heal their land." One of the contingencies for God to bring healing to the land is for us to turn from our wicked ways.

After David sinned with Bathsheba and the prophet Nathan brought his sin to his attention, David repented before the Lord, saying, "Restore unto me the joy of thy salvation; and uphold me with thy free spirit" (Ps. 51:12). A major key to having joy in your salvation is letting go of the flesh and allowing God's Spirit to lead you. You can't expect God to bless and restore you if you don't honor Him.

God manifests His power.

After the children of Israel cut away their flesh, God's power showed up. Again we read in Joshua 5:

> Now when Joshua was near Jericho, he looked up and saw a man standing in front of him with a drawn sword in his hand. Joshua went up to him and asked, "Are you for us or for our enemies?"
>
> "Neither," he replied, "but as commander of the army of the LORD I have now come." Then Joshua fell facedown to the ground in reverence, and asked him, "What message does my Lord have for his servant?" The commander of the LORD's army replied, "Take off your sandals, for the place where you are standing is holy." And Joshua did so.
>
> —JOSHUA 5:13–15, NIV

This passage is telling us that when we denounce rejection, lust, fear, anxiety, or anything else that is not like God, we open the way for a supernatural manifestation of God's power.

God restores our position.

No one wants to live in a condemned building. Yet people spend their lives thinking they will never be good enough for God to use them. Second Corinthians 7:10 tells us that "godly sorrow worketh repentance to salvation not to be repented of: but the sorrow of the world worketh death." Worldly sorrow is dangerous because it causes hopelessness. And if you are punishing yourself for something you have repented of, you won't be able to move to the next level in God. But godly sorrow knows how to ask God for forgiveness and then get back in position.

God wants to restore your position. In the Book of Numbers,

Moses's brother Aaron and his sister Miriam conspired against Moses. Miriam was a prophetess, and both she and Aaron were upset with Moses because of the woman He chose to marry. So they began complaining about their brother.

God got upset and caused Miriam to develop a form of leprosy. Moses attempted to intervene on her behalf, but God explained to him that Miriam had to suffer the consequences of her actions.

> But the LORD said to Moses, "If her father had but spit in her face, would she not bear her shame for seven days? Let her be shut up for seven days outside the camp, and afterward she may be received again."
> —NUMBERS 12:14, NASB

We see at the end of this verse that Miriam was to be received again. That means God gave Miriam back her position. God is a restorer.

Sometimes our trials are the result of other people's choices, and sometimes they're no one's fault; it's just life. But sometimes our pain is due to our own choices, as it was with Miriam. In life we make mistakes, and we may have to experience the consequences of those choices. The Bible says clearly: whom the Lord loves, He chastises. He brings correction to us when we need it because He loves us. But God does not throw us away. If someone gave you a balled-up one hundred-dollar bill, would you throw it in the trash? No. You would take the time to straighten it out so it could be used. Well, that is what our Father does for us. God will not throw us away; He will make every crooked place straight, and then He will use us for His glory.

We all know the story of the prodigal son. There were two sons living with their father. The youngest son decided to leave home and take his inheritance. The Bible says he lived a riotous life, squandered all his inheritance, and found himself in the gutter. In that low place he decided to return home, and when he did, his father put shoes on his feet, a regal robe on his back, and a ring of authority on his finger. You see, restoration in the kingdom is not second-class citizenship, but first-class sonship! God wants you back in your position. He loves you.

God's power extends beyond simply restoring our position. God also wants to restore our lost time and finances. Have you ever said, "I gave them the best years of my life" or "They ruined my life"? If you've ever made these statements, be sure not to say them ever again. You don't have to live in the pain or mistakes of yesterday. God will restore your time and finances.

God restores lost time.

God will restore your lost years. Joel 2:25 says, "And I will restore to you the years that the locust hath eaten, the cankerworm, and the caterpiller, and the palmerworm, my great army which I sent among you." How in the world can years be given back? How can they be restored to us?

In the Book of Ruth, Naomi and her husband were affluent in Israel. Times got tough due to famine, so they moved to Moab, and eventually Naomi's sons married Moabite women. Naomi's husband got sick and died, and later on her two sons died as well. With her husband and sons gone, Naomi decided to return to Israel, and her daughter-in-law Ruth accompanied her. The community was in disbelief when they saw how broken Naomi looked when she returned. She made no attempt to hide her grief and told everyone to call her bitter (*Mara*).

But God is a restorer. With some guidance from Naomi, Ruth married a wealthy man named Boaz, and they had a son named Obed, who just happened to be the grandfather of King David.

> Then the women said to Naomi, "Blessed is the LORD who has not left you without a redeemer today, and may his name become famous in Israel. May he also be to you a restorer of life and a sustainer of your old age; for your daughter-in-law, who loves you and is better to you than seven sons, has given birth to him." Then Naomi took the child and laid him in her lap, and became his nurse. The neighbor women gave him a name, saying, "A son has been born to Naomi!" So they named him Obed. He is the father of Jesse, the father of David.
> —RUTH 4:14–17, NASB

Not only did Naomi gain a wealthy son-in-law and a grandson, but the Bible says Ruth was better to her than seven sons (Ruth 4:14–17). God restored Naomi's lost years to the point that she was able to nurse her own grandchild.

God restores lost years. I watched God restore the seven years in my life the enemy had devoured. He restored me to ministry, He restored my hope and joy in Him, and He even restored me financially. It was simply amazing.

God restores lost finances.

God wants to restore us in every way, including financially. In 2 Kings 8 a woman who had befriended Elisha the prophet ultimately had to leave Israel because of a seven-year famine in the land. When the seven years ended, she returned home and found that others had taken over her land. She appealed to the king of Israel to intervene, and when she did, it just so happened that Gehazi, Elisha's former servant, was talking with the king and recounting all the miracles Elisha had performed. One of those miracles included raising this woman's son from the dead.

The king was amazed that while Gehazi was telling him that story, the woman showed up in his court. The king asked her if the story was true, and she said it was. So the king ordered her land to be returned, along with any profit those who had taken it had made in the last seven years. Thus she was restored; both her possessions and the lost wages were returned *in a day*!

The promise of God is that if we sacrifice for Him, all will be restored to us, and we will be paid back with compounded interest. When Peter reminded Jesus that the disciples had left everything to follow Him, Jesus said:

> Yes...and you won't regret it. No one who has sacrificed home, spouse, brothers and sisters, parents, children—whatever—will lose out. It will all come back multiplied many times over in your lifetime. And then the bonus of eternal life!
> —LUKE 18:29–30, THE MESSAGE

The Lord is faithful to restore. When I became a single parent, the weight of providing for our household became mine. I diligently worked my network marketing business and did well. Our bills were paid, and I was careful to sow seed into the kingdom of God, even though there wasn't much left over each month after everything was paid. Then, in time, I received a settlement that restored my finances even beyond where they were before. I didn't even know that money existed. But God knows the end from the beginning.

God knew all along that after we had lost so much and after all the financial sacrifices we had made, He would restore.

I often wonder what would have happened if I had yielded to the pressure to give up on God. I would have lost so much! That is why we must trust God even when we don't understand what He is doing. God can and will restore—with interest.

Ride Out the Storms

God is a restorer, but people can miss their opportunity for restoration because they allow the storms of life to distract them. Often when God gives you an assignment to do something, a storm will arise to hinder you. Don't let the storm stop you. The dictionary defines a storm as "a disturbance of the atmosphere marked by wind and usually by rain, snow, hail, sleet,...and lightning." It also can mean "a disturbed or agitated state" or "a sudden or violent commotion."[2]

Just as it is in the natural, so is it in the spirit. Storms take place all over the earth. All of us experience them. No one is exempt. It rains on the just and the unjust (Matt. 5:45). Storms can and will come to us in all shapes and sizes.

In the natural, the speed and intensity of the wind are what determine how a weather event is classified. With that in mind, I want to share with you three categories of storms that come into our lives because weathering these storms is key to experiencing restoration.

Category 1: The test

This is the first level of a storm. It causes concern but no real damage. In Mark 4 a storm arose while Jesus was asleep on a boat. He woke up and simply rebuked it, saying, "Peace, be still. And the wind ceased" (Mark 4:39).

A test is a storm that you know can bring calamity, yet in

the midst of it you have a supernatural confidence that everything is going to be all right. If I had to choose a storm to go through, this would be the one. This type of storm could be a flat tire or a late payment for a bill. The problem is solvable but still causes some anxiety. It's the kind of storm where you can see the light at the end of the tunnel and know that everything is going to be OK.

When you face this kind of storm, rest in the knowledge that Jesus is not dead; He is yet alive, and He still declares, "Peace be still," over our storms. In Isaiah 37 the Israelites were facing a threat from the Assyrians. The Bible says, "Then the angel of the LORD went out and put to death a hundred and eighty-five thousand in the Assyrian camp. When the people got up the next morning—there were all the dead bodies!" (v. 36, NIV). When you're in the midst of a test, know that God will fight for you.

While the Israelites were sleeping, the angel of the Lord put to death 185,000 Assyrians. Just as Jesus slept on the boat while the storm was raging, He wants us to rest in Him in the midst of our test. He wants us to know that even when we think He is sleeping, He is fighting for us.

Category 2: The faith builder

The second type of storm will test your faith because you won't know how you're going to get through it. You are well aware that God is your anchor and your source, but the high winds become a major distraction. God allows this to happen, and He will step in at 11:59 p.m., just seconds before the midnight hour, because He wants us to learn to trust Him.

In Matthew 14 the disciples were on yet another boat while a storm was raging, and this time Jesus was not with them. But check out what happened:

And in the fourth watch of the night Jesus went
unto them, walking on the sea. And when the disciples saw him walking on the sea, they were troubled,
saying, It is a spirit; and they cried out for fear. But
straightway Jesus spake unto them, saying, Be of
good cheer; it is I; be not afraid. And Peter answered
him and said, Lord, if it be thou, bid me come unto
thee on the water. And he said, Come. And when
Peter was come down out of the ship, he walked on
the water, to go to Jesus. But when he saw the wind
boisterous, he was afraid; and beginning to sink,
he cried, saying, Lord, save me. And immediately
Jesus stretched forth his hand, and caught him, and
said unto him, O thou of little faith, wherefore didst
thou doubt? And when they were come into the ship,
the wind ceased.

—MATTHEW 14:25–32

Storms can either make us or break us, depending on how
we respond. Trials, tragedies, and tribulations can be either
a stepping-stone or a stumbling block toward our destiny,
depending on our heart's response.

My dear friend Edith Young turned her storm into a
stepping-stone. She was ecstatic that she was going to be a
home owner. But on the day of her closing, the bank still
hadn't sent the money for her loan, and the closing was
scheduled for 4:00 p.m.

Knowing her situation, I asked her if she was going to
reschedule, and she said, "No, the Lord said today is the
closing." When noon came around, I called her to see if the
money had come in, and she said no. But she stood by faith
that all would be well. This continued for most of the after-
noon. I'd call her, and she would tell me no, the money hadn't

come in. At 3:30 p.m. there was still no money. Yet Edith was still standing in faith, and she was not moved. Miraculously, at 3:50 p.m., the money came, and she closed at 4:00 p.m., as God said she would!

That situation easily could have been a stumbling block for Edith, but she chose to use it as a stepping-stone to exercise her faith. As I watched her go through that experience, I had to examine my faith. I probably would have unwittingly chosen the stumbling block, rescheduled the closing, and then blamed it on the devil. We all have a choice. No one wants to face storms in life, but storms can round off our rough edges.

Category 3: The war zone

This storm is the least desired, but it yields the most benefit. When you weather this storm, you will come out stronger, blessed, and walking in a greater anointing. This storm is major, and some people think God would never allow us to go through something so intense. But Daniel in the lions' den, the Hebrew boys in the fiery furnace, Job, and many others in Scripture can attest that God doesn't always stop the storms that come, even the worst of them. Instead He teaches us how to maneuver through them. As Romans 8:31 says, "If God be for us, who can be against us?"

The apostle Paul had firsthand experience with a *war zone* storm.

> Now when much time was spent, and when sailing was now dangerous, because the fast was now already past, Paul admonished them, and said unto them, Sirs, I perceive that this voyage will be with hurt and much damage, not only of the lading and ship,

but also of our lives.... But not long after there arose
against it a tempestuous wind, called Euroclydon.
—Acts 27:9–10, 14

In this passage Paul was going to Rome by way of the
Mediterranean Sea. He was likely traveling in October or
November, which is considered the worst time of the year to
travel that route because of the storms. An angel appeared to
Paul and warned him that they were going to run aground
and be shipwrecked. Paul also had an unction in his spirit
about the trip. In other words, he knew this was a storm that
would not be stopped. Yikes!

God certainly does allow major storms in our lives, but
why? It's because they can propel us to where He wants us to
be. God had an incredible plan to bless Paul and bring people
to salvation on the island of Malta. And He used the storm to
propel Paul to exactly the right place at the right time.

Storms can take us places where we never thought we
would go. I never in a million years thought I would be part
of a network marketing business because I don't have the
high-energy, charismatic personality most successful network marketers have. But when a *war zone* storm came and
devastated my income, I ventured out to do something I
never thought I would do, and it yielded more income than
the job I lost.

God will use storms to take us to another level in Him,
but the enemy will use storms too if you let him. In each
of the storms discussed in this chapter, the people were in
a boat because they needed to get somewhere. The opposition doesn't want you to get to your destination because he
knows God wants to display His power on the other side of
the storm.

In Luke 8 Jesus and His disciples were on a boat headed to the other side of the lake. Jesus had fallen asleep when a storm hit, and the boat started filling with water. The disciples feared they were going to sink, so they woke Jesus up. When they did, He simply rebuked the waves, and the storm immediately calmed down. Why so much drama just to cross over a lake? It's because when they arrived on the other side, Jesus would heal a man with a legion of demons, and a whole community would witness the power of God.

God used the storm as a catalyst to manifest His power, and He does the same with the storms we face.

> For God, who commanded the light to shine out of darkness, hath shined in our hearts, to give the light of the knowledge of the glory of God in the face of Jesus Christ. But we have this treasure in earthen vessels, that the excellency of the power may be of God, and not of us. We are troubled on every side, yet not distressed; we are perplexed, but not in despair; persecuted, but not forsaken; cast down, but not destroyed; always bearing about in the body the dying of the Lord Jesus, that the life also of Jesus might be made manifest in our body. For we which live are always delivered unto death for Jesus' sake, that the life also of Jesus might be made manifest in our mortal flesh....For our light affliction, which is but for a moment, worketh for us a far more exceeding and eternal weight of glory; while we look not at the things which are seen, but at the things which are not seen: for the things which are seen are temporal; but the things which are not seen are eternal.
> —2 CORINTHIANS 4:6–11, 17–18

Yes! The hope of this passage is an anchor in times of storms. I get excited when I think about the fact that God loves us so much that He will use our times of trouble to make Christ manifest. My question to you is, has Christ ever been made manifest in you? The only way that will happen is if you allow Him to take the captain's seat when the storms of life come. You may be wondering, "How do I let God take control when everything is out of control?" That's a good question. I want to spend the rest of this chapter giving you five strategies for maneuvering through a storm.

Maneuver Through the Storm

A maneuver is "a military or naval movement; an armed forces training exercise."[3] It is a procedure or method of warfare, often involving evasive movements. Within Paul's shipwreck experience in Acts 27 and 28 are five clear insights that will help us maneuver through life's storms so we won't miss the time of our restoration.

1. Lighten the load (Acts 27:18).

During a major storm you must lighten the load. Paul and his shipmates needed to get rid of any unnecessary weight. Isn't that so true of us too? The Bible tells us in Hebrews 12:1 that we must get rid of any weight that will hinder us. Unnecessary weight can be friends who are not edifying you, ungodly relationships or activities, frivolous spending, or feelings of resentment, bitterness, or fear. We must let them go. We must do our part so God can do His part.

2. Let go, and let God (Acts 27:40).

Most control freaks don't like this step in maneuvering through the storm. Faith is a necessary component to get through tough times. In Acts 27:40 we see that the wind took the crew where it needed to go. In other words, God was leading the ship. There are many people who think they can stop storms without God. I must say, they are sadly delusional. You can't stop a storm with your looks, charisma, or gifts. It is God in and through you who stops the storms of life.

We read in 2 Corinthians 4:16 that "though our outward man perish, yet the inward man is renewed day by day." Let's be real. Relationships decay, looks fade, people change, and the things we thought would last forever sometimes don't. That's OK. We don't lose hope because we don't put our hope in people or superficial things that decay. When our hope is in God's ability to lead us where we need to go even in the midst of the storm, we will be able to ride it out with smiles on our faces and peace in our hearts. This is what it means to let go and let God—it's making a conscious decision to walk in faith and not in our own strength.

3. Seek God's specific plan for your storm (Acts 27:43).

> But the centurion, willing to save Paul, kept them from their purpose; and commanded that they which could swim should cast themselves first into the sea, and get to land: And the rest, some on boards, and some on broken pieces of the ship. And so it came to pass, that they escaped all safe to land.
> —ACTS 27:43–44

God may lead you through the storm along a different path than others. Please don't make the mistake of trying to maneuver the way someone else did because you admire his results. God has made you uniquely, and it is imperative that you hear His voice for your specific need. Acts 27:44 shows us that some maneuvered through the storm by using boards or broken pieces of the ship to work their way to land. They all used different means but made it safely to the same destination. Trust God to show you the path He has for you and face the storm in the power of the Lord of hosts. (See 1 Samuel 17:45.)

4. Shake off the snakes (Acts 28:6).

Miraculously everyone survived the shipwreck and was warmly received by those on the island of Malta. But while Paul was placing wood on the campfire, a viper bit him and fastened itself on his hand. For Paul to survive such a terrible storm only to be bitten by a snake on the island made the people think he surely must have done something awful because God was going to punish him one way or another.

> Howbeit they looked when he should have swollen,
> or fallen down dead suddenly: but after they had
> looked a great while, and saw no harm come to him,
> they changed their minds, and said that he was a god.
> —ACTS 28:6

Paul didn't allow fear to set in when the snake bit him; he simply shook it off. That's what God wants us to do when a spiritual viper attacks during the storm. He doesn't want us to complain about it or rehearse it in our mind. He wants us to respond to the enemy as if he is a nonfactor. Shake off the snakes, and focus on the Redeemer.

An interesting fact is that the snake was driven out of its hiding place because of the heat generated from the fire, and that's when it bit Paul. Many people never experience the bite of the enemy because they aren't doing anything to agitate him. When you are kingdom-minded and you care about the salvation of souls, face it; you will agitate the enemy, and you shouldn't be surprised when he bites. But please understand that "no weapon that is formed against [you] shall prosper" (Isa. 54:17).

Paul was on assignment from God, and I am sure he thought, "Please. A snake bite? Is that all?" After everything Paul had seen—the miracles, the demons cast out, the angelic visitations—his anointing must have been off the charts! The snake had no power to intimidate Paul. But here's the best part: the same power and anointing that rested on Paul's life is available to you today. Don't let the snakes intimidate you; shake them off!

5. Let God use the storm (Acts 28:8).

God wants to use the storm to manifest Christ to others—so let Him!

> And it came to pass, that the father of Publius lay sick of a fever and of a bloody flux: to whom Paul entered in, and prayed, and laid his hands on him, and healed him. So when this was done, others also, which had diseases in the island, came, and were healed.
>
> —Acts 28:8–9

The trial of the storm led Paul to a remote island. The viper attack opened the people's hearts to receive from Paul, and as a result Christ was made manifest to them. What a mighty God we serve. The people wanted Paul to pray for them. They didn't have to be pumped up or compelled; they were drawn to the Christ in Paul.

Then, after the people experienced Christ's power on the island of Malta, God restored Paul:

> Who also honoured us with many honours; and when we departed, they laded us with such things as were necessary. And after three months we departed in a ship of Alexandria, which had wintered in the isle, whose sign was Castor and Pollux.
> —ACTS 28:10–11

Notice what this verse tells us: *God restored and replenished Paul in the place where the storm led him.* Acts 28:10 says the people gave much honor to Paul and loaded him down with things necessary for his travels. This is my testimony all the way! I am a recipient of God's restoration after a devastating storm. As Ephesians 3:20 says, God "is able to do exceeding abundantly above all that we ask or think, according to the power that worketh in us."

God is still loading me down with His benefits. But I do have battle scars. Paul was bitten by the snake and got a battle scar, but it led to the great victory of seeing an entire village changed by the power of Christ.

Your storms are not random; God has a plan to see you through the storm, manifest Christ, and then restore and replenish you. When you go through a storm—and we all will—I encourage you to meditate on Psalm 3. You even may want to memorize it and make it your prayer to the Lord. (I have quoted it in the King James Version, but use whatever translation you choose):

> Lord, how are they increased that trouble me! many are they that rise up against me. Many there be which say of my soul, There is no help for him in

God. Selah. But thou, O LORD, art a shield for me; my glory, and the lifter up of mine head. I cried unto the LORD with my voice, and he heard me out of his holy hill. Selah. I laid me down and slept; I awaked; for the LORD sustained me. I will not be afraid of ten thousands of people, that have set themselves against me round about. Arise, O LORD; save me, O my God: for thou hast smitten all mine enemies upon the cheek bone; thou hast broken the teeth of the ungodly. Salvation belongeth unto the LORD: thy blessing is upon thy people.

Don't lose heart in the storm, and don't try to manage it in your strength. Allow God to take the captain's seat. If you do, He will maneuver you through any storm, great or small, and restore and replenish you.

Chapter 7

KEEP MOVING FORWARD

———————— ❧ ————————

I T'S NOT EASY to move forward in life when you've gone through years of trials and hardships. It's not easy to press on toward your purpose when you don't see how the pieces of your puzzle fit together. But you can't wait until your way is clear to start moving forward. You must make up your mind to put your hope in God and choose to follow Him even if you can't see where He's taking you or how He will bring to pass what He has spoken to you.

What has God promised you? What has He put in your heart to do? Don't put those things on the shelf. Don't believe the lie that you are too old to accomplish your goals. Don't settle for less in life because you think your window of opportunity has passed. Move toward what God has promised you in Jesus's name. With each step you'll see God's bringing the pieces of your puzzle together for His glory.

To move forward through seven years of trials and testing, I had to stay positive. There was no room for me to develop a critical spirit. A critical spirit is different from a critical mind. People with a critical mind offer constructive critiques that build up and encourage. Those with a critical spirit tear down and destroy. The critical spirit is not of God; it is of the flesh because it produces condemnation of others. People can lose their hope and confidence if they're constantly criticized for everything they do. They even may begin to think they're not good enough to achieve their dreams and goals.

I've found that wounded people can be the most critical of others. The saying is true: hurt people hurt people. Those who don't handle the negative seasons in their lives correctly can become bitter and resentful and end up hurting others through their pain. Don't let the doubters slow you down. Ignore them, and trust God. "Be ye stedfast, unmoveable, always abounding in the work of the Lord, forasmuch as ye know that your labour is not in vain in the Lord" (1 Cor. 15:58). Your labor is never in vain when you move toward the purposes of God. He will accomplish His will through you by His grace.

I was encouraged to continue standing on the Word of God and not focus on my pain, and the encouragement I was given made it possible for me to cross the finish line. In time I was able to see that each of my puzzle pieces was necessary for God to accomplish His purposes in my life. As Psalm 119:71 says, "It was good for me to be afflicted so that I might learn [His] decrees" (NIV). I kept it moving despite the suffering, and boy, did I gain life lessons!

MOVE WITH GOD

The Bible tells us that Enoch walked with God (Gen. 5:24), and it says, "Noah was a righteous man, blameless among the people of his time, and he walked faithfully with God" (Gen. 6:9, NIV). Noah and Enoch are the only two men about whom this is said. Walking with God means moving in the same direction in which He is moving. It's not moving ahead of God or lagging behind Him; it means keeping in step with God. Both Noah and Enoch had amazing intimacy with God. We'll take a closer look at Enoch in chapter 10. Right now I want to focus on Noah.

Noah lived ten long generations after Adam and Eve. He was declared righteous in God's sight because he was a consistent believer even though the world around him thought he was crazy. Noah was called "blameless," which doesn't mean he was literally perfect but that he was not contaminated. Noah was not contaminated by the wickedness of his day, and the wickedness was great. The Bible tells us that "every imagination of the thoughts of [mankind's] heart was only evil continually" (Gen. 6:5). It was so bad the Lord was sorry He had made man.

But Noah "found grace in the eyes of the LORD" because he was "a just man and perfect in his generations, and Noah walked with God" (Gen. 6:8–9). Noah was different from those around him, and he didn't try to change to fit in. He embraced his difference and moved with God. And because Noah moved with God against the odds, he accomplished a seemingly impossible feat.

Noah is an incredible example for us to follow. Philippians 2:14–15 says if we live out our faith, we will shine as the stars in the universe amid a crooked and depraved generation. Noah's life reminds us that being different, having an unusual assignment, or feeling lonely doesn't give us permission not to move with God.

One of the biggest causes of my discouragement was the fact that I lost so much in such a short period of time. After my divorce I lost my home and the ministry I had cofounded and served in for nearly fifteen years. After the death of my ex-husband I felt that my children and I lost the ability to mourn Zachery's death privately and manage our legacy without interference. Honestly, it would have been easier for me just to stop and not move forward. But I had to teach my children how to move forward, which took years of walking them through the grief of our broken marriage and then the grief of their father's death while I myself was still grieving.

Genesis 6:22 tells us that "Noah did everything just as God commanded him" (NIV; see also Genesis 7:5). When you choose to do what you know is right or to obey a specific command the Lord has given you, you inevitably will move forward.

A lot of people try to blame others for the fact that they're motionless. They think that because they have been wronged, they have a valid excuse to stop moving toward their purpose. Well, in Noah's day human beings had become so corrupt the Lord "regretted that he had made [them]" (Gen. 6:6, NIV), and He decided to wipe them from the face of the earth and start over. You can't get much more evil than that. Yet God called Noah in the midst of the evil. Your job is not to focus on the injustice you have experienced (or are experiencing). Instead you are to focus on the God who is our solution. Let me tell you, it is not an easy task to walk by faith and not by sight. But obedience is the first step.

In Genesis 6:13–15 (NIV) God said to Noah:

> I am going to put an end to all people, for the earth is filled with violence because of them. I am surely going to destroy both them and the earth. So make yourself an ark of cypress wood; make rooms in it and coat it with pitch inside and out. This is how you are to build it: The ark is to be three hundred cubits [450 feet] long, fifty cubits [75 feet] wide and thirty cubits [45 feet] high.

Can you imagine what Noah must have thought? Noah was asked to build a wooden structure almost four stories high, longer than a football field, and as wide as half a football field. God also asked Noah to fill the structure with two of every kind of bird and animal, male and female, as well as food of all kinds. Despite the massive assignment and the massive opposition, Noah chose to move forward.

Noah faced unbelievable scrutiny from his neighbors. He was constantly mocked and ridiculed. When you have a big dream in your heart, you may be scorned if the pieces of your puzzle don't look the way people think they should. You may know that God called you to start a business, but you have not obtained your MBA. Or, like me, you may be a woman God called to establish and pastor a church. Those who believe it's not biblical for a single woman to pastor a large ministry have ostracized me. Those who believe I should have stayed married to a man who was repeatedly unfaithful have distanced themselves from me as well. But I was able to move forward because I was certain God was with me. You must stand confidently on what God has said to you as well, and keep moving forward.

It took Noah 120 years to build the ark. It's unbelievable to me that each morning, Noah got up to build something that had never been built before in preparation for something he had never seen before—rain. My seven years is like two minutes in comparison to Noah's journey. However, his tenacity is our example. Noah never gave up. He kept it moving even though people devalued him and his journey was incredibly long.

In the end, Noah's decision not to give up saved his family. The Bible says when the rain fell, every living thing on earth was wiped out. Only Noah and those with him on the ark survived (Gen. 7:11–12, 23).

Noah warned anyone who would listen that the flood was coming, but he was ignored. When the floods came, Noah was vindicated. Have you shared your dream with others, only to have them disregard or ridicule you? Don't be discouraged. When your dream is still in its infancy, you may be snubbed. Will you stand against the opposition and ridicule of others?

We must take a stand, as Noah did, to save our families.

> As it was in the days of Noah, so it will be at the coming of the Son of Man. For in the days before the flood, people were eating and drinking, marrying and giving in marriage, up to the day Noah entered the ark; and they knew nothing about what would happen until the flood came and took them all away. That is how it will be at the coming of the Son of Man.
> —MATTHEW 24:37–39, NIV

Just as the door of the ark remained open, so is God beckoning the lost with His Spirit. Some laugh at the lifestyle of the believer and continue in wickedness. But we must be like Noah, who "being warned of God of things not seen as yet, moved with fear, prepared an ark to the saving of his house; by the which he condemned the world, and became heir of the righteousness which is by faith" (Heb. 11:7).

GET MOVING

You never know what God will do once you get up and start moving. In 2 Kings 7 the Arameans had besieged Samaria, which was experiencing a severe famine. One day four leprous men who were sitting at the gate of Samaria said to one another, "Why do we sit here until we die?" (2 Kings 7:3, NASB). They figured if they went into the city, surely they would die of starvation because of the famine. If they stayed where they were, they would die also. But if they went to the camp of their enemy the Arameans, they had a fifty-fifty chance of surviving. They might be killed, or their lives might be spared, and they would be given food. So they got up and went to the Arameans' camp.

The Lord used their act to perform a miracle. As they moved toward the camp, the Lord caused their steps to sound like those of a mighty army. The Arameans fled in fear, and the lepers were able to plunder their camp. All of Israel was saved because four men decided to get up and get moving.

It's important to realize that this miracle was for more than these four men, and even for more than the people of Samaria. The day before, the prophet Elisha declared that the famine would be over the next day. God used the lepers' act to perform His word. What would have happened if the four lepers had decided to become complacent, resentful, or bitter in their circumstance and refused to move forward? The breakthrough God had planned for His people wouldn't have come to pass. If we don't get up and move forward, we could miss the miracle God has for us—and possibly the opportunity to bless others.

Abraham didn't give up but kept it moving even though it seemed too late for his promise to manifest.

> Against all hope, Abraham in hope believed and so became the father of many nations, just as it had been said to him, "So shall your offspring be." Without weakening in his faith, he faced the fact

that his body was as good as dead—since he was about a hundred years old—and that Sarah's womb was also dead. Yet he did not waver through unbelief regarding the promise of God, but was strengthened in his faith and gave glory to God, being fully persuaded that God had power to do what he had promised.

—Romans 4:18–21, niv

Face it. Opposition will come. When you start moving toward your dreams, people will mock you and discourage you, but stay in your position. Some of you will go back to school, and people will say you are too old. Some will venture out into new business endeavors, and people will say you are not qualified. Others will start a ministry, and people will say you're not anointed, or you will purchase a home, and people will say you don't have enough money. Instead of listening to the naysayers, take time to study the Word of God and the many examples in Scripture of people who kept moving forward despite the odds.

In John 6 the disciples were trying to move forward in the dark amid raging seas:

The sea began to be stirred up because a strong wind was blowing. Then, when they had rowed about three or four miles, they saw Jesus walking on the sea and drawing near to the boat; and they were frightened. But He said to them, "It is I; do not be afraid." So they were willing to receive Him into the boat, and immediately the boat was at the land to which they were going.

—John 6:16–21, nasb

Notice that the passage did not say anything about them stopping or turning back. They were moving forward even though conditions were difficult. When they saw Jesus walking on the sea, they were willing to let Him on board once they realized it was really Him. I love what happened next: "And immediately the boat was at the land." They were just suddenly where they were going. That sounds like redeeming the time to me. Your season may be dark, and seas may be raging in your life, but never give up! Let Jesus in, and He will move you full throttle to your destination.

A throttle is a device for controlling the flow of fuel or power to an engine. To move full throttle is to do something completely without restraint or at full speed. Colossians 4:5 tells us to "live wisely among those who are not believers, and make the most of every opportunity" (NLT). We belong to God. What a great testimony to those who are not believers if we are able to move over every obstacle and speed bump for His glory.

To restrain is to hold something back from action, "to limit, restrict, or keep [something] under control." It means "to deprive of liberty [as by] arrest; to moderate or limit the force, effect, development, or full exercise of."[1] To be restrained is to be in some type of imprisonment or bondage that hinders your forward movement. The word *bondage* comes from the Greek word *douleuó*, which means to be a slave to something, whether literal or figurative, involuntary or voluntary.[2]

God gives us the power to push past the restraints of this life. In the church world, when we hear the word *bondage*, we think of drugs, alcohol, sexual perversion, and the like. But the Bible says in 2 Peter 2:19 that "people are slaves to whatever has mastered them" (NIV). That master could be pride, jealousy, control, or fear. Ask yourself, "What is restraining me from maximizing opportunities?"

Sometimes the hindrances are not obvious. It may be a spouse who won't trust God or an adult child who lives in your basement and refuses to step out on his own. It could be a good idea that isn't a God idea and thus hinders your progress.

Some people go through life never recognizing the hindrances keeping them from progressing. It's like they're driving with their parking brake on, never realizing that they have the power to move faster. My dear friend has a younger brother. When they were growing up, she used to beat him up and treat him pretty badly. My friend was around five feet tall and petite. Her brother grew to be close to six feet tall and was stocky, but even as they grew, he allowed her to continue to beat him up. Then one day he realized he was stronger than she was, and he fought back. My friend never touched him again.

In life we often wonder why we are moving so slowly. Oftentimes it's not God's doing; it's because we're driving with our parking brakes of fear, procrastination, or doubt on. Take the limits off, and let God propel you forward. The psalmist said, "Search me, O God, and know my heart; try me and know my anxious thoughts" (Ps. 139:23, NASB). And 1 John 4:1 says to "test the spirits to see whether they are from God, because many false prophets have gone out into the world" (MEV). These scriptures give us instructions for conducting a diagnostic test that would reveal anything that might cause us to stop or break down en route to our promise.

There will be pit stops as you move toward your purpose. Normally a vehicle stops in the pit during a race for refueling, new tires, and mechanical adjustments. Sometimes pit stops require a change in drivers. The pit can strengthen us for the journey.

God utilizes ordinary people to do extraordinary things. Throughout the Word of God we see how God used unlikely people to accomplish magnificent exploits. Could God be seeking to move you forward to a greater assignment? Have you ever thought that maybe some of your dilemmas are actually catalysts for a great move of God in your life? Looking back over my life, I see a pattern of God's using my incomprehensible journey to lead me to a place of greater strength and peace! I can now look at life's hindrances with optimism and faith.

If you think you've drifted *away from* rather than *toward* your dreams and goals in life, I want to encourage you. Demotion can become promotion when you stay in motion toward God. What looks to us like digression may be preparation for exaltation. Joseph is a prime example. He was betrayed by his natural brothers, put in a pit, sold into slavery, and then thrown into prison. I am sure few of those who knew him in prison imagined he would one day become second-in-command in Egypt.

After God took him from the pit to the palace, Joseph told his brothers, "You intended to harm me, but God intended it for good to accomplish what is now being done, the saving of many lives" (Gen. 50:20, NIV). Joseph was a teenager when he dreamed that his family would bow down to him. That dream came to pass, but he had to go on a painful thirteen-year journey. Joseph was seventeen when his brothers threw him in the pit, thirty when he was made an overseer of Egypt's resources, thirty-nine when he was reunited with his brothers, and forty-one when he revealed himself to his family.³ What a journey! Joseph lived to be 110 and saw his great-grandchildren. I am sure those thirteen years of pain paled in comparison to his happy ending. Joseph kept it moving, and his dream became a reality.

God increases our anointing in the pit. Joseph had a literal pit stop when his brothers threw him into one. But that is where God began to align him with His plans for his life and prepare Joseph for the palace. Practically speaking, your pit stop may be losing your job of many years. But in the unemployment pit stop God may give you a plan for a business or invention. You may be in the divorce pit stop, where the Holy Spirit brings healing and teaches you to love yourself. Or maybe you're in the foreclosure pit stop, where God wants to teach you His principles on giving, stewardship, and restoration. God does not want to put new wine in old wineskins because the new wine will burst the old wineskins. So He'll use the pit stop to renew your mind and repair your spirit so you don't give up when things get rough, and you'll be prepared for the new things He plans to do in you.

CONFRONT THE ENEMY

There are pit stops that are orchestrated by God, and then there are hindrances that come straight from the pit of hell. Satan wants to bring your progress to a screeching halt, and if he can't get you to sabotage yourself with your own doubts, he'll look for another way to derail your progress. You can't take this threat lightly. You must confront the enemy as soon as he rears his ugly head.

Jesus was a confronter. He would take something that was out of order and immediately put it in order. When Peter began to tell Jesus, "O Lord, You cannot go to the cross; I love You too much," Jesus immediately said, "Get behind me, Satan," because Jesus did not want anything to get into His spirit that was against the will of God. (See Matthew 16:13–23.)

Jesus confronted the enemy because He knew that if Satan got an inch, he would take a mile. If Satan can get just a little bit of his foot in the door, he will worm his way into your life and begin to tear you down to keep you from moving forward. We must understand, as Jesus did, that if we resist the devil, he will flee.

The Bible says James and John were preparing a place in Samaria for Jesus to go minister, and the Samaritan people wouldn't receive Jesus. This caused James and John to get angry, and they said, "Jesus, let's cast down fire on these people." Jesus said, "You don't know what manner of spirit you speak of. I have not come to destroy people. I have come to save them." (See Luke 9:51–56.)

Immediately Jesus spoke order to disorder, and that's the mentality we must have. If we don't confront things, we'll start to complain about them instead. When we complain about our marriage, children, jobs, and so on, we're exalting the enemy. Jesus never exalted the enemy. He never complained about the enemy. He exposed the enemy. He exposed the enemy so we could understand the devil's strategies and guard ourselves against them.

How do we protect ourselves from the enemy's devices? Mark 16:17 says, "In my name shall they cast out devils." I love that scripture. That tells me I have authority in Jesus's name. He said, "Shall they..." That means we *will* do it. Declare right now, "I will cast the devil out of my life in the name of Jesus!"

Many of us are afraid of the enemy. When I was a child, I didn't want to even say the word *Satan*. I was scared to say *devil.* I didn't like the color red, and I didn't want to get a receipt that said $6.66. But eventually I had to ask myself who had the authority, the enemy or me. If you're intimidated by the enemy, you must begin to understand your realm of authority as a child of God. We sometimes give the enemy too much power over us. We need to take back everything the devil stole and move forward in our God-given assignment.

Second Corinthians 2:11 tells us not to be ignorant of Satan's devices. This is because if we, as believers, do not understand the enemy's tactics, he will gain the advantage over us. The enemy fights in many ways, but the two devices I want to focus on in this chapter are temptation and the wiles of the devil.

1. Temptation

The Bible says Jesus was tempted in the wilderness for forty days. The enemy said, "Turn the stone to bread, cast Yourself off this mountain, worship me, and I'll give You the 'kingdoms of the world.'" (See Matthew 4:1–11.) The enemy was blatant in his efforts to tempt Jesus. But Jesus knew He was the One with more power and thus was able to resist Satan's enticements. Jesus said we would do greater works than He did. And the Holy Spirit that raised Jesus from the dead is the same Holy Spirit who dwells within us. We have been given authority over the enemy (Luke 10:19).

Having said that, it's important that you know your limits. We all have temptations that we must flee from instead of trying to resist them. If you just got saved and were delivered from drug abuse, should you go witnessing down on the corners where they sell drugs? No. If you just got saved and are committed to abstaining from premarital sex, should you go try to witness to your old flames, where the spirit of lust is quite strong? No. We're talking about the obvious.

James 1:14 says, "But every man is tempted, when he is drawn away of his own lust, and enticed." The enemy wants to put a hook in something within you so he can get you to fall into sin. That's all temptation is—a hook. But 2 Peter 2:9 says, "The Lord knoweth how to deliver the godly out of temptations." You can be saved and full of the Holy Ghost and still be tempted. But the Bible says the Lord knows how to deliver you out of temptation. Let Him guide you.

Maybe you know all too well how it feels to fall into temptation and go backward instead of forward in God. You don't have to live in condemnation. Once you ask God to forgive you, God can take you from that position of lowliness and cause you to still fulfill your purpose. It's a trick of the enemy to tell you it's over because of mistakes you've made in the past. It's a trick of the enemy to say you'll never accomplish what God said you would.

If you feel condemnation in your heart, we come against it right now in the name of Jesus. I speak freedom, liberty, and increase into your life right now in the name of Jesus. I break the chains the enemy has used to shackle you. You will get to the next level. You will make it. You will be a success. Don't let the enemy trick you any longer.

2. The wiles of the devil

The wiles of the devil are different from temptation. A wile is a scheme that is hidden. It's made to deceive you. It's designed to cause you to fall into sin unwittingly. Have you ever heard someone say, "If only I could be a fly on the wall..."? Why would anyone want to do that? Because a fly can be there, and nobody notices it. That's how the enemy wants to come into your life. He wants to come in without your even knowing it.

When the apostle Paul was doing the work of the ministry, there was a woman who kept following him around, saying, "Oh, glory be to God. You are so great, Paul." She was flattering him, but Paul wasn't given to vanity. Something rose up in him, and a red flag went up in Paul's spirit. He realized the woman was operating under a spirit of witchcraft, so he turned around, and he rebuked her. (See Acts 16:16–18.)

Initially that spirit of divination wasn't obvious. It was a scheme of the enemy. We have to understand that everything that shines isn't gold. Just because it looks and sounds good doesn't mean it is good.

A common wile of the enemy is to have an attractive new coworker strike up a friendship with you. The person talks nicer to you than your spouse does, is better groomed than your spouse, and compliments you more often than your spouse does. This new coworker doesn't nag you and makes you feel at ease. By now the Holy Spirit has warned you, but you let it slide. Before you know it, you find yourself watching this coworker throughout the day and looking forward to striking up a conversation.

You see, it started small, but the next thing you know, you are eating lunch with a friend, and here comes this coworker you've been fantasizing about. You all eat lunch together, and then eventually you find yourself eating lunch alone with that coworker. You tell yourself there's nothing going on, but you know what you feel. Even if no one else knows, you do. You're dreaming about the person at night. You're thinking about that individual when you're getting dressed in the morning. That coworker is a wile of the devil meant to bring sin into your life and break up your family.

SWAT THAT FLY

Another name for Satan is Beelzebub, which means "lord of the flies." It is our responsibility to SWAT that fly. In the military, SWAT stands for Special Weapons and Tactics. When there's a fly around, if you try to hit it with your hand or a rolled-up newspaper, the fly will sense the air pressure changing because your hand is solid and will move before you get close to it. But a flyswatter has a pattern of little holes in it that keeps the fly from sensing the pressure change. So when you get close to it, the fly doesn't know you're there, and you can kill it.

God wants to give us special weapons to attack the enemy. We have to be aggressive against him. The enemy traditionally has sought us out, but God wants us to get to the place where we can go after him. We must SWAT him before he attacks us and keeps us from moving forward into our purpose. We have authority over the devil and the power to stand firm amid attack. We just need to keep our spiritual eyes open and utilize the special weapons and strategies we have been given to defeat the enemy.

No longer can the enemy sit on me. No longer will he keep me immobilized. No longer will he take my joy with his annoying antics. The enemy won't take my peace or the finances God has given me. He won't rob me or hinder my progress because I know I can come against him. I know that Luke 10:19 says God has given me authority over all the power of the enemy.

So what are some of the ways we can SWAT the enemy so he can't stop us from moving forward in life? First, we must put on the full armor of God, as Ephesians 6:13–17 (ESV) explains.

> Therefore take up the whole armor of God, that you
> may be able to withstand in the evil day, and having
> done all, to stand firm. Stand therefore, having fas-
> tened on the belt of truth, and having put on the
> breastplate of righteousness, and, as shoes for your
> feet, having put on the readiness given by the gospel
> of peace. In all circumstances take up the shield of
> faith, with which you can extinguish all the flaming
> darts of the evil one; and take the helmet of salvation,
> and the sword of the Spirit, which is the word of God.

What I want to concentrate on is the phrase "Therefore
take up," particularly the words "take up." If on the day of
battle a soldier had not taken up his full armor, he would
be unprepared to fight the enemy. The "evil day" discussed
in this verse is the day of severe tests or trials; it is when the
devil would seek to attack us most fiercely. We never know
when these kinds of crises will occur, which is why we must
always be ready. Honestly there are days when you're so tired
and overwhelmed by life, you barely have enough strength to
take up anything. Yet you are still obligated to draw strength
from God so you will be ready for whatever the enemy tries
to throw your way.[4]

So many of us are weary and tired, but God says, "I'm
going to give you enough strength for you to pick up that
shield of faith and that sword of the Spirit so you can stand.
I know you're a little wobbly right now, but once you get
that armor on, you can establish yourself and stand strong
against the enemy."

In the remainder of this chapter I want to share three disciplines that will empower you to stand strong in God and
SWAT that fly.

1. Confess the Word.

Of all the weapons at our disposal, the most important one is prayer. When you get up in the morning, if you have no strength to pray or push or pursue God, just do one thing. Take one step. That one step may be saying the name of Jesus or saying, "Thank You, God." To move mountains, all you need is faith the size of the grain of a mustard seed. But you have to give God something to work with. If you can just do one thing, the next thing you know, you'll have ministering angels in the room to comfort, keep, and help you. And where there was no energy, there will be strength. But you have to take the step first. God will not force you.

The Bible says, "Cast not away therefore your confidence, which hath great recompence of reward" (Heb. 10:35). Trust that God will do what He says. Have confidence that He will watch over His word to perform it (Jer. 1:12). If God told you your body would be healed, don't be afraid to declare, "My doctor may not believe it, but healing is on the way. The test looks bad, but God told me I was going to be healed." In your confidence there is strength. Standing in confidence on God's Word will increase your faith.

You don't have to complicate this; the weapon of prayer isn't difficult to use. Prayer is saying, "God, I need Your help today. You said I was going to make it. I believe that, but I don't feel like it's true. Yet Your Word says, 'Let the weak say, I am strong' (Joel 3:10), so that's what I choose to do." That's how you pray. You don't have to know a thousand scriptures. God looks at your heart.

2. Worship.

The second weapon is found in Ephesians 5:18–19: "And be not drunk with wine, wherein is excess; but be filled with the Spirit; speaking to yourselves in psalms and hymns and spiritual songs, singing and making melody in your heart to the Lord." You see, when Jesus went into the wilderness in Matthew 4, the Bible says He was full of the Holy Ghost. We also have to be full of the Spirit of God. If we are full of the Holy Spirit, then when something else tries to get in, there's no more room. Tell the enemy, "I'm full. I have God in me. You're not getting in here."

King David understood that. He went through attack after attack, but the Bible says he wrote and sang songs to the Lord. He kept his spirit lifted by singing. Worship the Lord, and you will see God move on your behalf. The Bible says He inhabits the praises of His people (Ps. 22:3). That means when you start praising and worshipping Him, He shows up! His presence will fill the room.

To speak melodies to God as Ephesians 5 describes, you just begin to pray what's on your heart. And if you don't have the words to say, start praying in the Spirit. That's why it's important to get filled with the Holy Ghost with the evidence of speaking in tongues, because when you don't know what to pray, guess what? The Holy Spirit knows what to say. When you allow the Holy Spirit to pray through you, you'll feel lighter. That heaviness you once felt will leave, and you will feel better. You'll feel as if you can make it, as if you can see light at the end of the tunnel.

3. Forgive.

The third weapon is found in James 5:16: "Confess your faults one to another, and pray one for another, that ye may be healed. The effectual fervent prayer of a righteous man availeth much." This kind of unceasing prayer will prevail over your circumstances and give you strength. But your prayers won't avail much if you have unforgiveness in your heart. If you have bitterness in your heart, if you're still gossiping and treating folk bad while you're praying, your prayers won't avail much until you forgive those individuals.

Forgiveness can be difficult, but God will strengthen you. Your heart will catch up with your mouth. Keep speaking your forgiveness, and your heart will manifest that reality. After Zachery's death my heart ached for my children. I was really upset with the board of New Destiny Christian Center because I felt the members' dealings with my children showed little respect. If I had allowed my heart to stay upset, bitterness and resentment would have been sure to enter. But I began saying, "I forgive them." I began saying, "I pray they will allow the Holy Spirit to lead them. I pray they walk in the spirit of truth." The more I said those things with my mouth, the more my heart came into agreement. When you are walking in forgiveness toward those who have hurt you, you will be able to realize it really wasn't about those people; the enemy was just using them to get to you.

As you walk in forgiveness, God will make you powerful in the spirit. When you use the weapons of God and begin to SWAT the enemy, every time the devil comes with a temptation or wile, you can pray, you can worship, you can declare the Word, you can forgive, and you can love and show compassion.

Using God's weapons instead of your own allows His grace to cover your life. His grace and favor are like insect repellent to the lord of the flies. When the enemy comes near you, he screams. Demons begin to tremble. They see a greater anointing on your life because you moved forward to God when you didn't feel like it, you forgave when your flesh was screaming for you to hold on to bitterness, and you chose to pray when it seemed as if you had no prayer left in you. When you use the strategies of God, you will be able to wage an aggressive attack against the enemy without his sensing you coming.

When you choose to seek God instead of giving in to distractions, God can trust you with more responsibility in the spirit. He can trust you to carry a greater measure of supernatural power. The Bible says we will do greater works than Jesus did (John 14:11–13). Why aren't we doing those greater works? Because the enemy has lied to us, and we have believed him. Every time you begin to feel rejection and anger, every time you begin to feel as if you're not worth much, every time you feel as if you can't press forward, shout at the top of your voice, "Devil, you are a liar! I am beautiful. God has made me wonderful, and I will accomplish everything God has given me to do. I may have messed up, but God has forgiven me. I backslid, but God has restored me and brought me to the front. I'm no longer living in condemnation." As you declare the truth out of your mouth, God will begin to manifest what you thought would never come to pass.

Forward movement takes commitment and dedication. Today your puzzle may be ambiguous, and you are unclear of what God wants to accomplish in your life. Beloved, be encouraged. If you keep moving forward with the knowledge you have, you will reach your destination and be a blessing to others. Don't give up in the pain and suffering. Keep moving forward no matter what obstacles you may face.

Chapter 8

DOUBLE HONOR
FOR YOUR SHAME

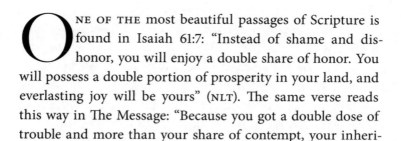

ONE OF THE most beautiful passages of Scripture is found in Isaiah 61:7: "Instead of shame and dishonor, you will enjoy a double share of honor. You will possess a double portion of prosperity in your land, and everlasting joy will be yours" (NLT). The same verse reads this way in The Message: "Because you got a double dose of trouble and more than your share of contempt, your inheritance in the land will be doubled and your joy go on forever."

It can be difficult to believe that for our shame God will give us double honor. That just doesn't make sense. It seems more logical to think God will give healing or peace in place of shame. But the scripture says we will enjoy a double share of honor and possess a double portion of prosperity in our land.

Some of the final problematic pieces to your puzzle will begin to make sense once you begin to glimpse how God wants to use them to bring increase in your life. That's when my puzzle started to come into focus, when I saw that God wanted to prosper me in ministry and even cause me to bear fruit as a business owner. For my shame He gave me double honor and prospered me in the place where His Spirit had led me.

Over the years I've spoken to countless men and women who live with shame on a daily basis. Shame is a feeling of disgrace or regret, and it can come in many forms. Pastors of churches with a handful of members and no increase in sight may feel the shame of barrenness. Entrepreneurs who struggle to keep their businesses open may feel the shame of failure. Divorcées may feel ashamed that their marriage ended, while single people may feel shame because they are not in a relationship, especially if the enemy whispers to them that no one ever will want to be with them.

Shame is a demonic device that leaves us feeling disgraced and unworthy. In Psalm 44:15–16 we get an idea of how shame works. The psalmist said, "My dishonor is continually before me, and the shame of my face has covered me, because of the voice of him who reproaches and reviles, because of the enemy and the avenger" (NKJV). Shame changes the way we see ourselves.

But the Bible says God will give us double for our shame. How does He do that?

I believe that God gives us an anointing to receive a double portion as we serve. In 2 Kings 2 the prophet Elijah asked his apprentice, Elisha, what he could do for him before he was taken from the earth. Elisha replied that he wanted a double portion of the anointing on Elijah's life. The prophet replied: "That's a hard one!...But if you're watching when I'm taken from you, you'll get what you've asked for. But only if you're watching" (2 Kings 2:10, THE MESSAGE).

Considering all that Elijah had walked through—he was

the one who humiliated the prophets of Baal on Mount Carmel when God sent fire from heaven and their god did not—I don't believe it was a hard thing for him to give Elisha a double portion of his anointing. That was the custom of the Old Testament. When a father or mentor died, the mantle would fall on the next person in line. When Elijah said this was a hard thing, I believe he was warning Elisha that carrying a double portion of the supernatural power of God wouldn't be a walk in the park.

After Elijah promised to give him a double portion if he saw Elijah when he was taken to heaven, Elisha wouldn't even let the prophet out of his sight. Elisha was committed to receiving all God had for him.

> And so it happened. They were walking along and talking. Suddenly a chariot and horses of fire came between them and Elijah went up in a whirlwind to heaven. Elisha saw it all and shouted, "My father, my father! You—the chariot and cavalry of Israel!" When he could no longer see anything, he grabbed his robe and ripped it to pieces. Then he picked up Elijah's cloak that had fallen from him, returned to the shore of the Jordan, and stood there. He took Elijah's cloak—all that was left of Elijah!—and hit the river with it, saying, "Now where is the GOD of Elijah? Where is he?" When he struck the water, the river divided and Elisha walked through. The guild of prophets from Jericho saw the whole thing from where they were standing. They said, "The spirit of Elijah lives in Elisha!" They welcomed and honored him.
>
> —2 KINGS 2:11–15, THE MESSAGE

Bible scholars say that when Elisha died, he had completed fifteen miracles, while Elijah had performed eight. But a short while after Elisha died, a young man was resurrected when his body was thrown into Elisha's tomb and touched the dead prophet's bones. (See 2 Kings 13:20–21.) That brought the number of miracles to sixteen—a true double portion.

It is interesting to see how the other prophets began to show Elisha respect after he received Elijah's mantle. The Bible says the sons of the prophets saw the spirit of Elijah on Elisha, and they bowed down. The anointing of God is not to impress the world; He gives it to us so we can accomplish His purpose in the earth. God allows you to go through tests and trials that are neither quick nor easy because of the undeniable anointing they will produce in your life.

POSITIONED TO RECEIVE

Let's look again at Isaiah 61:7 (NLT):

> Instead of shame and dishonor, you will enjoy a double share of honor. You will possess a double portion of prosperity in your land, and everlasting joy will be yours.

Did you catch that? There was a contingency on how the children of Israel would receive the double portion of prosperity. It would be in their land. Your land is the spiritual place God ordained for you to receive your inheritance, and it is through obedience that you position yourself in that place. God led me to launch a new church, and He has blessed me in that place. Had I decided to return to corporate America in disobedience to God's command, I couldn't have expected to receive the double portion God had for me because I would have been out of position. You cannot receive double honor if you won't be obedient and position yourself where God wants you.

Zechariah 9:12 says, "Come back to the place of safety, all you prisoners who still have hope! I promise this very day that I will repay two blessings for each of your troubles" (NLT). In Zechariah 9 the children of Israel had been going through a difficult season that was painful for them. But through all the trials they had to endure, they kept their hope in God, and God promised to repay them two blessings for each trouble. In other words, He gave them double for their trouble when they returned to the place of safety. For their shame God gave them double honor.

In chapter 6 we briefly discussed the dreaded pieces of Ruth's puzzle. Losing a husband, brother-in-law, and father-in-law would be a devastating blow for any woman, especially in Bible days. During that time women were considered property and were effectively second-class citizens. With no men left in Ruth's immediate family, her future looked bleak because she had no one to provide for her. But after much heartache and struggle, Ruth experienced restoration. She probably grew to love every piece of her puzzle, including the dreaded ones, because they led her to her new husband, her child, and her happiness. What's more, she ended up in the lineage of King David and Jesus, which I'd definitely consider double honor.

An even closer look at Ruth's story allows us to see how God redeemed her from shame and gave her double honor. Ruth's story begins with a man named Elimelek leading his wife, Naomi, and their two sons to Moab to escape famine. After Elimelek died, his sons Mahlon and Kilion married Moabite women named Ruth and Orpah.

Ruth is clearly identified as a Moabite in Ruth 1:4. This may not seem like a big deal until you go back to Deuteronomy 23:3, where it says, "No Ammonite or Moabite or any of their descendants may enter the assembly of the LORD, not even in the tenth generation" (NIV). Also, Nehemiah 13:1 says, "On that day the Book of Moses was read aloud in the hearing of the people and there it was found written that no Ammonite or Moabite should ever be admitted into the assembly of God" (NIV).

The Ammonites and Moabites were not permitted to enter the assembly of the Israelites because of a time when the Israelites set up camp in the land of the Moabites. The King of Moab thought the Israelites would overthrow his kingdom because they were so numerous. So he hired the prophet Balaam to curse the Israelites. (See Numbers 22 and Deuteronomy 23:3–4.)

Furthermore the Bible tells us Moab and Ammon were born of incest to Lot and his elder and younger daughters, respectively, after the destruction of Sodom and Gomorrah. (See Genesis 19:36–38.) As if that weren't enough, their forefather Lot was given to selfishness. In Genesis 13:7 there was strife between Lot's herdsmen and his uncle Abram's herdsmen, so Abram (whom God later renamed Abraham) decided that he and Lot should separate. Abram let Lot choose whatever land he wanted, and Lot chose the best territory. Abram was Lot's uncle, but he had treated Lot as a son. Lot should have said, "No, Uncle Abram. You've been too good to me. I will take what is left over." But that's not what he did. He took the best for himself.

So as you can see, Ruth's bloodline was riddled with the shame of selfishness and incest, and she was not supposed to enter the assembly of God. How then did Ruth become the great-grandmother of King David? Why did God give Ruth double honor for her shame?

A LOYAL LOVE

The answer begins in Ruth 1:8. Naomi said to her two daughters-in-law, "Go, return each of you to her mother's house" (ESV). Then Naomi said something very key: "May the LORD deal kindly with you, as you have dealt with the dead [a reference to their husbands] and with me" (Ruth 1:8, ESV).

The word translated "kindly" in this verse is the Hebrew word *hesed*. This term stands for several ideas—love, mercy, grace, kindness—but it is perhaps best translated "loyal love." Wrapped up within this word are all the positive attributes of God. As one commentator explained it, *hesed* is "a quality that moves someone to act for the benefit of someone else without considering, 'What's in it for me?'"[1]

Hesed epitomizes the love God shows us, as Lamentations 3:22–23 declares: "The steadfast love [*hesed*] of the LORD never ceases; his mercies never come to an end; they are new every morning; great is your faithfulness" (ESV). And it is one of the things God requires of us as His people, as Micah 6:8 states: "What does the LORD require of you, but to do justice and to love kindness [*hesed*], and to walk humbly with your God?" (MEV). *Hesed* is one of the Lord's most treasured characteristics, and this is the kind of love Ruth demonstrated to Naomi.

> And Ruth said, Intreat me not to leave thee, or to return from following after thee: for whither thou goest, I will go; and where thou lodgest, I will lodge: thy people shall be my people, and thy God my God: Where thou diest, will I die, and there will I

be buried: the LORD do so to me, and more also, if
ought but death part thee and me.

—RUTH 1:16–17

Both Ruth and Orpah left with Naomi when she decided
to return to the land of Judah, but when Naomi urged them
to go back to their families in Moab, Orpah eventually gave
in. She kissed Naomi good-bye and returned to her people
and her gods. Ruth, however, refused to leave and accompanied Naomi all the way to Bethlehem. Ruth displayed *hesed*, a
loyal love that made her embrace Naomi as her responsibility.

Hesed is the same kind of love the good Samaritan showed
the wounded traveler who had been attacked by thieves.
The man had been ignored by a priest and a Levite, but the
Samaritan "went to him, and bound up his wounds, pouring
in oil and wine, and set him on his own beast, and brought
him to an inn, and took care of him" (Luke 10:34). The Jews
treated Samaritans poorly, but this man still made the unfor-
tunate fellow his responsibility, just as Ruth made Naomi her
responsibility.

Again we see Ruth demonstrating *hesed* in Ruth 2:2–3:

> And Ruth the Moabitess said unto Naomi, Let me
> now go to the field, and glean ears of corn after him
> in whose sight I shall find grace. And she said unto
> her, Go, my daughter. And she went, and came, and
> gleaned in the field after the reapers: and her hap
> was to light on a part of the field belonging unto
> Boaz, who was of the kindred of Elimelech.

Naomi was a wealthy and influential woman when she
left Bethlehem with her husband and two sons. She returned
a poor, brokenhearted, childless widow. In fact, she was so

changed the women exclaimed, "Can this be Naomi?" (Ruth 1:19, NIV). By offering to do the gleaning, Ruth spared Naomi the humiliation of going among the poor in the fields, where she possibly would have been pitied and mocked.

I believe this is when the favor of God rested upon Ruth, for we see that Boaz was led to his field at the same time Ruth was there. One of Boaz's servants told him Ruth had been there all day and rested little (Ruth 2:7). And later, after Ruth made her desire to marry him known, Boaz said, "Blessed be thou of the LORD, my daughter: for thou hast shewed more kindness [*hesed*] in the latter end than at the beginning, inasmuch as thou followedst not young men, whether poor or rich" (Ruth 3:10).

The servant Elisha received a double portion from Elijah because he stayed with his mentor and saw him when he was caught up to heaven. Similarly Ruth displayed *hesed*, a loyal love, when she served Naomi, and I believe God blessed her for it.

Ruth converted to Judaism and held sacred the law of God. But it was her selfless acts of kindness and service toward Naomi—her *hesed*—that revealed her true devotion to the Lord. Today her dedication is highly regarded. The Book of Ruth traditionally is read during the Jewish festival of Shavuot, in part because her loyalty to Naomi symbolizes the faithfulness to the Torah that is expected of all Jewish people.[2]

As Ruth displayed *hesed*, loving and serving Naomi and her people, God positioned her for restoration. She was blessed with not only a husband but also a son, who became the grandfather of Israel's greatest king, David. And she is in the lineage of Jesus.

I think it's important to note that at no time in Ruth's

story do we see her focus on her past. It is possible that Ruth and her sister-in-law Orpah were Moabite princesses.[3] That may be one of the reasons Naomi told them to return to their own people. I have thought so many times about the days when I was married and being cared for by my husband. Oh, how I longed for a knight in shining armor to come and take my burdens away. I often would cry myself to sleep.

When I was married, I didn't carry the weight of responsibility I have today as a single mother and pastor. I long for simple things, such as not having to drive myself home after church on Sundays when I'm exhausted after preaching two services, not having to be responsible for all the bills, partnering with someone as a co-laborer in ministry, or having someone to sit with at conferences and not having to be a third wheel all the time. The memories of yesterday can be sweet, but you can't effectively move forward while you're looking in the rearview mirror.

Ruth experienced the shame of losing her husband, having to start over, and even being shunned because of her ethnicity. Oh, how I can relate to those puzzle pieces. I honestly can say I never felt humiliated, as most whose spouses have been unfaithful do. But I did feel the shame that others were dishing out to me—the shame of being divorced while in ministry and the shame of losing so much that I once had.

Yet looking back over my seven-year journey, I noticed a pattern. The more I exhibited *hesed* to others, the more my puzzle pieces started coming together.

Yes, in the midst of heartbreak, I still was serving others with the love of Jesus. When I first learned of Zachery's infidelity, in July 2007, we stood together and went through counseling. We sought help from several counselors, including one in Canada. Although word of his unfaithfulness was spreading, he didn't make a public statement until October of that year. Throughout that time I sought to show *hesed* and forgiveness in the midst of the devastation. When his continued infidelity was exposed to me, I had peace to move forward with my life unmarried.

After the divorce I felt ostracized by some of the leaders at New Destiny; few even called to see if I was OK. Meanwhile my heart broke as I saw the members and employees of New Destiny begin to scatter and a few of the employees ostracized. I was given a lump sum of money as part of the divorce settlement, but I was still in great financial need. I had just started my network marketing business, and I didn't have much money left over after paying my bills. But still I chose to use money from the lump sum to help some employees with their mortgage payments and medical bills. It wasn't my duty to assist them, but I took it as my responsibility. I believe that God took notice.

As my business was becoming more successful, I thought of relocating to Scottsdale, Arizona, to get as far away from Orlando as possible. But God called me to stay and establish a church here. I trusted Him while trembling. I didn't go back to corporate America as Orpah went back to her previous life. I forged ahead into uncharted territory as Ruth did.

Miraculously the Holy Spirit drew people to our church mostly by word of mouth. Again, *hesed* was the key to seeing God's blessing on the ministry as the launch team faithfully served the members. Anyone who has started a ministry from the ground up knows it requires sacrifice. You take it as your responsibility to serve the members and the community. I believe in being a servant leader. The only celebrity in our church is Jesus.

During the long legal battles before and after Zachery's

death, I had every opportunity to stand on my soapbox and share all the details of our family's struggles. But *hesed* wouldn't allow me. I still loved Zachery, and I learned how to forgive him. I desired the best for him as the father of my children, and I held my peace. Zachery accomplished many great things during his lifetime, and I pray that is never forgotten. My hope is that other ministry families can avoid what we went through, which is why I desired to launch a center for families that are struggling with infidelity, substance abuse, burnout, and so on.

It is remaining in love—*hesed*—that begins the process of bringing everything together. It is showing this loyal love for God and others that allows you to overcome hardships and suffering and see your puzzle finally begin to take shape. My seven years of struggle were in the hands of a loving God the entire time; my test was to exhibit the same love in the midst of my circumstances.

Showing love is the starting point for all things coming together in your life. As 1 John 4:20 says, "If a man say, I love God, and hateth his brother, he is a liar: for he that loveth not his brother whom he hath seen, how can he love God whom he hath not seen?"

Ruth 4:13 tells us that Boaz and Ruth had a son whom they named Obed. After the child was born, the women of the city honored Naomi and called her blessed of the Lord. In the end, Ruth's puzzle pieces all came together to create a beautiful picture of God's redemptive power to turn shame into honor. For her shame Ruth was given a new husband and baby, and Naomi was once again part of a family.

God wants to turn your shame into honor too. It really doesn't matter how intricate or debilitating your circumstances are. Nothing is too hard for God.

While you're in the middle of your trial, God is waiting for you to exhibit *hesed*, the loyal love of God, which encompasses the fruit of the Spirit: "love, joy, peace, longsuffering, gentleness, goodness, faith, meekness, temperance" (Gal. 5:22–23). Matthew 5 paints a picture of how God begins to bring everything together when you learn to love this way. When you do this, God is able to mold you to fit the destiny He has for you.

> You have heard that it was said, "You shall love your neighbor (fellow man) and hate your enemy." But I say to you, love [that is, unselfishly seek the best or higher good for] your enemies and pray for those who persecute you, so that you may [show yourselves to] be the children of your Father who is in heaven; for He makes His sun rise on those who are evil and on those who are good, and makes the rain fall on the righteous [those who are morally upright] and the unrighteous [the unrepentant, those who oppose Him]. For if you love [only] those who love you, what reward do you have? Do not even the tax collectors do that? And if you greet only your brothers [wishing them God's blessing and peace], what more [than others] are you doing? Do not even the Gentiles [who do not know the Lord] do that? You, therefore, will be perfect [growing into spiritual maturity both in mind and character, actively integrating godly values into your daily life], as your heavenly Father is perfect.
>
> —MATTHEW 5:43–48, AMP

Matthew explains that maturity in mind, character, and spirit are a result of *hesed*. It is necessary to submit to God's maturation process if you want to possess double honor.

We can love the unlovable only by submitting to the Holy Spirit and by the grace of God. The Holy Spirit humbles us to become a servant, and His grace allows us to endure hardship. Loving others is the first step to seeing it all come together. The next step is patiently enduring.

A TEST OF ENDURANCE

Let's look at another woman, Rizpah. I talked about Rizpah in my book *When It All Falls Apart*, but from a different perspective. Joshua 9 tells us that Joshua made a peace treaty with the Gibeonites under false pretenses. The Gibeonites deceived the children of Israel by wearing old, worn-out clothes, which convinced Joshua that they were travelers from far away. Joshua granted them peace with an oath sworn by the Lord. But later Joshua found out they were neighbors, the Gibeonites with whom God had warned Israel not to make any treaties. The oath remained valid because it was sworn by the Lord, but Joshua made the Gibeonites woodcutters and water carriers.

Four hundred years later, when Saul was king of Israel, he didn't regard the oath made between Israel and the Gibeonites, and he massacred many of them (2 Sam. 21:1–2). As a result, there was a famine. David asked the Gibeonites how he could appease the blood guilt that was causing the famine, and the Gibeonites replied that he could hand over seven of Saul's male descendants to be hanged. David took two sons Saul had with his concubine Rizpah and the five sons of Saul's daughter Michal and delivered them into the hands of the Gibeonites, who hanged all seven of them.

This brings us to Rizpah. Her name means hot or glowing stone.[4] This probably had to do with her physical beauty as the king's concubine. A concubine was considered the property of the king and could be passed from one king to another. The concubines were given special privileges because many of them were expensive investments. They were pampered, lived in luxurious surroundings, and were served by many attendants. At a moment's notice any one of them could be sent for by the king, so they were groomed constantly.

Rizpah was a woman used to the finer things of life. She and her children were supposed to be protected. How could this happen? The Law said it was not permissible to put children to death for the sins of their parents, and vice versa, but each would be held responsible for his own sin (Deut. 24:16). Add to that the fact that the treaty between Joshua and the Gibeonites was made more than four hundred years earlier, and it had been several years since Saul had sinned against the Gibeonites. Rizpah must have wondered, "Why now? Why my sons, and why me?"

When negative things happen in your life due to circumstances out of your control, how do you respond? Some people get angry at God and backslide. Some people go into a deep depression and stop moving forward. Some take it upon themselves to seek vengeance. Yet others are determined to overcome with God's help. I thought about doing all of the above, and I thank God I pursued the latter. Trusting and obeying God is the only path that leads to double honor.

After her sons were killed, Rizpah took sackcloth and spread it over herself on a rock and protected the bodies of her sons from the birds by day and animals by night for five or six months. The decaying bodies summoned vultures and wolves, yet Rizpah stood her ground to protect the bodies of her sons. Rizpah spent six months mourning her dead sons, and for six months she fought off wild animals day and night. If this was how much Rizpah loved her sons in death, I can only imagine how she loved them in life.

Rizpah was determined to protect her children. She didn't care about her privileged lifestyle when she was protecting her sons' bodies. She very well may have been hungry and exhausted, but nothing stopped her vigil. The community must have thought she had lost her mind, and they probably mocked and pitied her. But she didn't care what others thought of her. She never gave up. This brings me to a second element necessary to see God bring everything together: endurance.

Endurance is "the ability to do something difficult for a long time; the ability to deal with pain or suffering that continues for a long time; the quality of continuing for a long time; the ability to withstand hardship or adversity, especially the ability to sustain a prolonged stressful effort or activity [such as a marathon]."[5] Rizpah displayed a tremendous amount of endurance when she was protecting her sons.

You need endurance to see God bring it all together and release double honor for your shame. During those seven years of hardship and trials I was determined not to give up. Like Rizpah, I was motivated to press forward by my love for my children. I needed endurance when I was in the midst of legal battles, stress, financial lack, loneliness, and spiritual and physical exhaustion. When I would go away to attend conferences, oftentimes I would daydream about getting back to the hotel to get some sleep, and I would pray the speaker would end the service early. I didn't want to fellowship after the service; I just wanted to sleep.

I would think back to times when I wasn't so exhausted and wonder when the season of exhaustion and pressure would end. I am sure Rizpah didn't know how long she would stay there to protect her sons, but she endured.

I know several people who lost loved ones many years ago, and they're stuck in the past. They've left their deceased loved one's belongings exactly as they were before the person died. And their conversations still center around their deceased loved one. I know others who constantly talk about their college football days, their former corporate careers, or their past ministry exploits, but they seldom talk of anything current. At some point they stopped moving forward. Endurance pushes you to reach the finish line even when it's well out of your view.

People often would ask me, "How do you keep going despite the negative media, gossip, and unfair treatment?" I always would answer, "I didn't have any other choice." But one day a life coach who attends my church corrected me. She explained that we all have choices, even if one of our options is to do nothing.

I woke up one Sunday morning with severe abdominal pain. The church was only about a year old, and I didn't have anyone who could preach for me on such short notice. So I endured the pain and preached the service. Immediately after church I asked to be taken to the hospital. It turned out that I needed emergency surgery to remove my appendix. Boy, I didn't see that one coming!

Another time I accidentally tripped on a twenty-pound weight and broke two toes, one on each foot. (I still wonder how I managed to do that.) So I preached in slippers. I've taken red-eye flights from the West Coast and headed straight to church from the airport to preach with no sleep. I've endured grueling schedules, long days building my network marketing business, and then long nights caring for my children. God used each of these circumstances to build my endurance.

Of course, hindsight is twenty-twenty, and I realize now

that all my decisions may not have been the wisest. But my motto always has been, "Never let the devil see you sweat." God honored my determination to endure. The church continued to grow without advertisement, and before we knew it, we had five hundred members and two services on Sundays, and one service on Wednesdays. Even though it was difficult to find our church because it was located at the far back of the parking lot of an industrial strip plaza, people continued to come.

Eventually the ministry was able to pay me a salary, and I stopped working my other job. But as I mentioned earlier, just when I was beginning to exhale, God said it was time for our church to move, and around the same time, Zachery passed away.

I found myself meditating on Scripture to find the strength to persevere. I clung to the following verses, which I would encourage anyone who is going through hardship to meditate on:

> But in everything commending ourselves as servants of God, in much endurance, in afflictions, in hardships, in distresses, in beatings, in imprisonments, in tumults, in labors, in sleeplessness, in hunger, in purity, in knowledge, in patience, in kindness, in the Holy Spirit, in genuine love.
> —2 Corinthians 6:4–6, nasb

> And you have perseverance and have endured for My name's sake, and have not grown weary.
> —Revelation 2:3, nasb

> And not only this, but we also exult in our tribulations, knowing that tribulation brings about

perseverance; and perseverance, proven character; and proven character, hope.
—ROMANS 5:3–4, NASB

Blessed is a man who perseveres under trial; for once he has been approved, he will receive the crown of life which the Lord has promised to those who love Him.
—JAMES 1:12, NASB

Rizpah endured the inclement weather and wild animals to guard the bodies of her children. Eventually someone told King David of Rizpah's vigil, and her actions prompted him not only to give her sons a proper burial but also to gather the bones of Saul and Jonathan and bury them properly with Saul's father. And it was then that God was moved by prayer for the land. (See 2 Samuel 21:11–14.)

Rizpah's endurance also can be an example for those who are praying for situations that seem dead or impossible—a failing marriage or ministry, a foreclosure, a wayward child, a chronic illness, or an incurable disease. Don't give up. Endure. If you walk in love, maintain faith in God's promises, and remain steadfast in prayer and praise, you will get God's attention.

My children watched me love God and God's people in the midst of overwhelming pressure. Today they are not bitter or angry with God. They saw God provide for us when it looked as if we weren't going to make it. My endurance was a faith builder for my children. That deposit is eternal. As I remained faithful in love and endurance, God brought clarity to my puzzle, and He started bringing it all together for me and through me.

Chapter 9

DON'T RUN FROM GOD

———— ❧ ————

HAVE YOU EVER wanted to run away when the pressure of life was intense? I have. Ministry can be stressful. Parenting can be stressful. Life can be stressful. Sometimes I just want to escape.

In those times the Lord has reminded me He won't put more on me than I can bear because He knows it is common to man to run when the pressure is on. That's what Adam and Eve did in the Garden of Eden after they disobeyed God. They hid from His presence. And Moses fled to the desert after he killed an Egyptian soldier. What they didn't seem to realize was that they weren't just running from their problems; they were running from God Himself and the calling He had placed on their lives. Adam and Eve were created to be in fellowship with God, yet they were running from His presence. Moses was called to deliver his people from slavery, yet he was running from Egypt.[1]

Running from what God has called you to do never works. Just consider Jonah, who is perhaps the most famous escape artist in Scripture.

> Now the word of the LORD came unto Jonah the son of Amittai, saying, Arise, go to Nineveh, that great city, and cry against it; for their wickedness is come up before me. But Jonah rose up to flee unto Tarshish from the presence of the LORD, and went down to Joppa; and he found a ship going to Tarshish: so he paid the fare thereof, and went down into it, to go with them unto Tarshish from the presence of the LORD.
>
> —JONAH 1:1–3

Somehow Jonah thought he could hide from God by fleeing the city. It's like a toddler who hides under the covers and thinks his parents can't see him because he can't see them. Some people think they can hide from God in their homes by occupying themselves with their children's schedules and to-do lists. Others may try to hide from God by burying themselves in their work. Still others try to run from God in church. Yes, I said in church. They attend super-large churches so they can hide in the pews and not be held accountable for their attendance or participation.

The Bible says in Psalm 139:12, "Yea, the darkness hideth not from thee; but the night shineth as the day: the darkness and the light are both alike to thee." The psalmist David is saying God sees in the darkness as if it were the day. He knows exactly where we are at all times. Out of sight, out of mind is a common expression. We lose touch with people and forget about them. But God never forgets about you. He is always well aware of where you are in life, even when you are hiding from Him.

LOVE TRUTH

Some people choose to attend a church that does not preach the unadulterated Word of God because they do not want to be convicted and challenged to change. The Bible says in John 3:20, "For every one that doeth evil hateth the light, neither cometh to the light, lest his deeds should be reproved." And Jeremiah 23:29 says, "Is not my word like as a fire? saith the LORD; and like a hammer that breaketh the rock in pieces?" There are times when the truth is painful to hear, but if you are wise and truly want to grow and become all God wants you to be, you will allow the Holy Spirit to change you.

God's desire is to make you a better you. You may have been living your life thinking what God had for you was like the shape of a triangle, but after God's Word begins to enlighten you, you may realize it was really a circle. God doesn't just want to expose who you are; He wants to mold you into something new, something greater than you ever thought you could become.

Hebrews 4:12 says, "For the word of God is quick, and powerful, and sharper than any twoedged sword, piercing even to the dividing asunder of soul and spirit, and of the joints and marrow, and is a discerner of the thoughts and intents of the heart." If you really want to receive all God has for your life, you must commit to obey His command no matter how painful or inconvenient it is. Can you imagine living your life thinking you were a great person and everyone liked you, only to realize people are actually afraid of you because you're so domineering? That's painful. God's truth is not always easy to hear, and His commands aren't always easy to follow, but He has our best interest in mind. It is worth it to obey Him.

God told Jonah to go to Nineveh, a place that had become wicked in God's sight. And instead of doing what God said, Jonah hitched a ride on a boat headed to Tarshish, a city in the opposite direction of Nineveh. If you were ever in Sunday school, you probably know what happened next. A great storm came, threatening the life of everyone on the boat. Jonah knew the storm was brewing because of him, so he told the ship's crew to throw him overboard.

They didn't want to, but eventually they did as he asked, and Jonah was tossed into the water. But God didn't let Jonah drown. The Bible says he was swallowed up by a great fish and remained in the fish's belly for three days before being vomited onto dry ground. When he was back on land, Jonah stopped running from God, and when God told him a second time to go to Nineveh, "Jonah got up and went" (Jonah 3:3, MEV).

Jonah is an example we can look to when we want to run away from God's plan for our lives. Jonah was not a new believer or a minister in training. Jonah was a seasoned prophet and servant of the Lord. He was used to hearing the voice of God. The problem was, this time he didn't like what God said.

God told Jonah, "Arise, go to Nineveh, that great city, and cry against it; for their wickedness is come up before me" (Jonah 1:2). In The Living Bible's paraphrase, verse 2 says the wickedness of Nineveh "smell[ed] to highest heaven." But God told Jonah to go to that foul-smelling city and let its people know that if they didn't obey Him, they would be destroyed, but if they repented, God would save them.

Most people believe that Jonah didn't want to go to Nineveh because he was scared. But, in actuality, Jonah didn't want to go to Nineveh because he hated the people there. He didn't think they were deserving of God's mercy.

> But it displeased Jonah exceedingly, and he was very angry. And he prayed unto the LORD, and said, I pray thee, O LORD, was not this my saying, when I was yet in my country? Therefore I fled before unto Tarshish: for I knew that thou art a gracious God, and merciful, slow to anger, and of great kindness, and repentest thee of the evil. Therefore now, O LORD, take, I beseech thee, my life from me; for it is better for me to die than to live.
>   —JONAH 4:1–3

Jonah would have preferred to die than to see God show mercy to a people he despised. That's why he ran from the call of God. Have you ever wished God would judge your enemies harshly? Have you ever felt pleasure at the misfortune of someone you did not like? Remember, 2 Peter 3:9 tells us, "The Lord is not slow in keeping his promise, as some understand slowness. Instead he is patient with you, not wanting anyone to perish, but everyone to come to repentance" (NIV). This was a lesson I had to learn. God is love, and He loves the world; that is why He gave us Jesus. God's desire is for all to come into the saving knowledge of Jesus Christ, including people who have caused us much pain. It's not our job to tell God how to bring justice in our situation; it's our job to trust Him.

TRUST AND OBEY

I can identify with Jonah. I never wanted to be a single mom or a single senior pastor. Pastoring by myself was my Nineveh. I had been hurt by people within the church. After my ex-husband's infidelity came to light, and then after his death, I felt rejected by the church. In both instances God commanded me not to run *from* but *to* the house of God. The church is made up of imperfect people, but God is perfect. People should never get a pass to sin, hurt others, or cause reproach to the body of Christ. But if that does happen, they will reap the consequences of their actions. Our responsibility is to forgive them.

Initially I was tempted to have church at home with my children by watching a Christian television program and reading the Word with them. However, I knew that wasn't what God wanted for us. Hebrews 10:23–25 says:

> Let us hold fast the profession of our faith without wavering; (for he is faithful that promised;) And let us consider one another to provoke unto love and to good works: Not forsaking the assembling of ourselves together, as the manner of some is; but exhorting one another: and so much the more, as ye see the day approaching.

God wants us to gather as a corporate body of believers in His name. Church hurt is one of the worst emotional or spiritual hurts you may ever experience. As Proverbs 18:14 says, "A man's spirit will endure sickness, but a crushed spirit who can bear?" (ESV). It is not natural to go back to the place where you've experienced tremendous pain. But if God leads you to do so, He will honor your obedience and give you supernatural strength to overcome any hurt or pain you may experience.

We all have faced times when we did not want to do something we needed to do. Some people are terrified to speak publicly. Others can't imagine leading a class discussion, going to a foreign land, or forgiving someone. Your Nineveh is whatever God requires you to do that is outside your desire, comfort, or convenience. Will you be obedient to the call despite the discomfort? When God called me to pastor again, I cried until there were no more tears to cry. I gave Him a list of reasons I wasn't qualified for the position. But I knew my tears wouldn't move God; my obedience would. So I obeyed His command to go to my Nineveh, and I took the calling He placed on my life seriously.

I think if more people took seriously the fact that God holds pastors accountable for the souls of those they lead, the prospect of going into ministry would be much more sobering. I do not take my position of pastor lightly. Our church keeps our financial books open to all our tithing members. I seek God for my sermons, and I am dedicated to living God's principles. I understand that we are not saved by works but by grace, but I also understand that we must reverence our God and honor Him by the way we reverence the authority He has given us over others.

I take seriously the call of God on my life. And because I take my calling so seriously, I can tell you you're not always going to like what God tells you to do!

You may be thinking, "I'm not like Jonah. I'm not running from anything God called me to do." But remember, your Nineveh may not be so obvious. Nineveh is whatever pulls you out of your comfort zone in order to accomplish the will of God.

In the previous chapter I wrote of how God used love and endurance to start bringing all the arbitrary pieces of my puzzle together. He also used obedience. God requires your obedience. John 8:12 says, "Then spake Jesus again unto them, saying, I am the light of the world: he that followeth me shall not walk in darkness, but shall have the light of life."

When we make a decision to run from God or hide from His presence, we are like that toddler I mentioned at the beginning of this chapter, who has the covers over his head and thinks no one can see him. The spiritual covers over our heads cause us to walk in darkness. You may search for answers in the darkness, but you'll never find what you're looking for outside of God's light. Run to God's light so you can see how He is bringing everything together.

When Majestic Life was only a couple of years old, our former minister of music and his wife decided to take a sabbatical for the birth of their first child. I thought that was great, but I was left with no music director. I wasn't sure what I was going to do. I had to remember that our church was built on the Word of God, not hype or entertainment. I knew that as long as our worship was pure before the Lord, He would be pleased even if it didn't sound super great.

Our bass player, Lydell, and his wife, Noni, were in our music department. They were both faithful. Lydell saw the need for a new music director, and he came to me and said he would temporarily take the position until I found someone. I didn't even know he could play the keyboard or sing, and I found out later he led choirs previously when he was living in Alabama. Lydell is also a pastor's kid, so he understood the dynamics of a growing church.

Leading in music ministry was his Nineveh. He had been burned out in ministry and didn't want the responsibilities or challenges when he and his wife moved from Alabama to Orlando. *But God.* God knew Lydell's call and purpose in life, and it was impossible for him to hide. He obeyed God's voice, and he is still our minister of music.

I've been obedient to God's command to go to several Ninevehs in my life. Obedience is necessary for God to bring everything together. Your act of obedience is evidence that you trust God.

Psalm 139:7–10 reminds us that we cannot hide from God. "Where can I go from Your Spirit?" the psalmist asks. "Or where can I flee from Your presence? If I ascend into heaven, You are there; If I make my bed in hell, behold, You are there. If I take the wings of the morning, and dwell in the uttermost parts of the sea, even there Your hand shall lead me, and Your right hand shall hold me" (NKJV).

We might be able to run from God, but we can't hide from Him. We can hide from the pastor, we can hide from our spouses, we can hide from our children, and we can hide from our bosses, but we can't hide from God.

There Is Power in Repentance

I am sure Jonah thought everything was OK when he was running away from his purpose. For a while, perhaps when he happened upon the ship leaving for Tarshish, it seemed as if everything was going in his favor. Isn't that what we do? We start saying things such as, "God opened this door for me," or, "I'm walking in the blessings of God because the ship was waiting for me." Every door that opens is not from God.

Jonah easily was able to hop on a ship that was headed in the wrong direction. And his disobedience landed him in the belly of a big fish. That is the deception of the enemy. He will take you further than you want to go. If you let him get his foot in your door through your disobedience, He'll come in as an invited guest and make it difficult for you to get rid of him.

Take time to examine your life. Ask yourself, "Am I running from God? What is my Nineveh?" If the Lord shows you a Nineveh, surrender it to Him. Once you've identified your Nineveh, be sure to repent. The Bible says Jonah cried in distress while in the belly of that fish.

> "When I had lost all hope, I turned my thoughts once more to the Lord. And my earnest prayer went to you in your holy Temple. (Those who worship false gods have turned their backs on all the mercies waiting for them from the LORD!)
>
> "I will never worship anyone but you! For how can I thank you enough for all you have done? I will surely fulfill my promises. For my deliverance comes from the Lord alone."
>
> And the Lord ordered the fish to spit up Jonah on the beach, and it did.
>
> —JONAH 2:7–10, TLB

God is a God of second chances, but repentance is necessary for God to bring all the pieces together. Make things right with God, and He will get you back on course. Proverbs 19:20–21 says, "Hear counsel, and receive instruction, that thou mayest be wise in thy latter end. There are many devices in a man's heart; nevertheless the counsel of the LORD, that shall stand." Never think God doesn't see you or that you can somehow manipulate Him into doing what you want. Remember, God is long-suffering. You may think you have gotten away with your disobedience, but nothing gets past God.

Face it, God is omniscient. He knows everything! You might as well stop wasting time, and trust God from the get-go. Psalm 33:11 tells us, "The plans of the LORD stand firm

forever, the purposes of his heart through all generations"
(NIV). And we read in Isaiah 14:24, "The LORD Almighty
has sworn, 'Surely, as I have planned, so it will be, and as I
have purposed, so it will happen'" (NIV). When Jonah was in
the belly of that fish and had lost all hope, the Bible says he
turned his thoughts to God once more (Jonah 2:7). He realized he could never get away from God, so he repented and
finally stopped running from Him.

Unfortunately people mistakenly think they're doing God
a favor when they obey His commands. When Elijah was
called to fight that horrific battle against Jezebel and the
prophets of Baal at Mount Carmel, he fell into a deep depression, thinking he was the only prophet willing to stand for
God. God told Elijah that He had reserved seven thousand prophets who also had not bowed their knees to Baal
(1 Kings 19:18). In Romans 11:5 we read that even today "there
is a remnant according to the election of grace." In other
words, God's plan will be accomplished with or without you.

When Zachery passed, I initially assumed the vision God
had given us had died as well. God allowed me to see that
the vision God gave Zachery and me was still alive, and He
wanted it to come forth. Isaiah 55:11 says, "So shall my word
be that goeth forth out of my mouth: it shall not return unto
me void, but it shall accomplish that which I please, and it
shall prosper in the thing whereto I sent it." I realized that
God's will would be accomplished. I wasn't doing God any
favors by accepting the call; He was favoring me with the
opportunity to serve Him.

The first day Jonah preached in Nineveh, the people
repented. The king called a fast, and God accepted their
repentance and did not judge the city. Ironically Jonah was
angry that God didn't destroy Nineveh. Still hoping that God

would destroy the people, he sat outside to look at Nineveh. God provided a plant to shelter Jonah from the sun, and then He allowed a worm to destroy it. Jonah was even angry about the withered plant, and he told the Lord he wanted to die. "Then the Lord said, 'You feel sorry for yourself when your shelter is destroyed, though you did no work to put it there, and it is, at best, short-lived. And why shouldn't I feel sorry for a great city like Nineveh with its 120,000 people in utter spiritual darkness and all its cattle?'" (Jonah 4:10–11, TLB).

Don't allow life's trials to cause you to become hardened, as Jonah was. Remember, our mission is to win souls. Love, endurance, obedience, and repentance are required of us as God puts all the pieces together.

RUN TO THE WELL

Instead of running away from God, you should run to the well. The well symbolizes the source of God's healing, a place where you can be refreshed and renewed. The well is also a place where you can find clarity about your puzzle. A puzzle, by definition, is something that leaves you feeling confused or perplexed because you can't make sense of it. At the well God brings more pieces of your puzzle together by giving you answers and instructions. John 7:37–38 says, "On the last day, that great day of the feast, Jesus stood and cried out, saying, 'If anyone thirsts, let him come to Me and drink. He who believes in Me, as the Scripture has said, out of his heart will flow rivers of living water'" (NKJV).

When you accept Jesus Christ as your Lord and Savior, you have access to the gift of the Holy Spirit. The Holy Spirit will lead and guide you into all truth. When you go to the well of Jesus Christ and drink of Him, He gives you all you need to solve every puzzling piece of your life. It's at the well that your spirit, emotions, and body can be cleansed from your past mistakes. And it's at the well that God gives you a revelation of your purpose and hope for the journey. Run to the well that is Jesus Christ.

Correction at the well

One of the first encounters with God at a well is found in Genesis 16. You probably know the story of Abraham and Sarah (who at this point in Scripture still were called Abram and Sarai because God hadn't changed their names). God promised them they would have a son, even though Sarah was well beyond her childbearing years. But after they had waited for years and years and still there was no promised child, Sarah took matters into her own hands and gave her servant Hagar to Abraham as a second wife. Sarah wanted Hagar to bring forth a child and then call that child hers. But when Hagar found out she was pregnant, things didn't turn out quite the way Sarah had hoped.

> And Sarai said unto Abram, My wrong be upon thee: I have given my maid into thy bosom; and when she saw that she had conceived, I was despised in her eyes: the LORD judge between me and thee.
> —GENESIS 16:5

Abraham responded by saying, "Behold, thy maid is in thine hand; do to her as it pleaseth thee" (Gen. 16:6). So Sarah "dealt hardly with her"—so hardly that Hagar "fled from her face" (Gen. 16:6). Some believe Sarah physically attacked Hagar and told her to get out. Whatever happened, Hagar found herself pregnant and alone in the wilderness.

> And the angel of the LORD found her by a fountain of water in the wilderness, by the fountain in the way to Shur. And he said, Hagar, Sarai's maid, whence camest thou? and whither wilt thou go? And she said, I flee from the face of my mistress Sarai. And the angel of the LORD said unto her, Return to thy mistress, and submit thyself under her hands.
>
> —Genesis 16:7–9

While Hagar was at a well in the wilderness, the angel told her, "Go back and make things right. You were wrong. You did not need to flaunt your pregnancy to Sarah. Get back in there and submit to authority." Oftentimes we don't want to submit because our pride is wounded. When you run to the well, don't be surprised if you are given correction. The Word of God says, "Whom the LORD loves He corrects" (Prov. 3:12, NKJV). At the well God will show you yourself. God brought correction to Hagar's life. The angel revealed that the problem wasn't with Sarah; it was with Hagar. To make things right, Hagar had to humble herself, return, and submit to Sarah's authority.

Prophecy at the well

After the angel of the Lord corrected Hagar, he said to her, "Behold, thou art with child and shalt bear a son, and shalt call his name Ishmael; because the LORD hath heard thy affliction. And he will be a wild man; his hand will be against every man, and every man's hand against him; and he shall dwell in the presence of all his brethren" (Gen. 16:11–12).

Isn't it awesome that even in your messed-up situation, God will give you a word? God will give you a promise to hold on to even when you make a mistake. When you turn your focus back to the things of God and really submit yourself to

168

Him, He'll speak to you. That just shows you how much God loves you. He is there for you, and He wants you to fulfill your purpose.

We read in Ephesians, "Husbands, love your wives, even as Christ also loved the church, and gave himself for it; that he might sanctify and cleanse it with the washing of water by the word, that he might present it to himself a glorious church, not having spot, or wrinkle, or any such thing; but that it should be holy and without blemish" (Eph. 5:25–27). Jesus washes us with His Word. Hagar was given a word that encouraged her about her future. Even though she was still in the wilderness, it was the word about her future that made it easier for her to return. Jesus washes us with His Word so we are cleansed from reproach and we can have hope for our future.

Impartation and intimacy at the well

Hagar must have been relieved and comforted by the word of the Lord. The Bible says, "And she called the name of the LORD that spake unto her, Thou God seest me: for she said, Have I also here looked after him that seeth me?" (Gen. 16:13). The Living Bible says it this way: "Thereafter Hagar spoke of Jehovah—for it was he who appeared to her—as 'the God who looked upon me,' for she thought, 'I saw God and lived to tell it.' Later that well was named 'The Well of the Living One Who Sees Me'" (Gen. 16:13–14).

You see, there aren't too many people who can really see us. Sometimes people can't see who we really are because we're wearing masks. Some of us have tears rolling down our faces under our makeup, but we're smiling on the outside, and nobody really sees us. Nobody really understands the pain and the torment we experience in the late-night season. They don't know we're crying at night into our pillows. They don't know the pain is sometimes so unbearable that we feel as if we're going to suffocate. They don't understand all that because all they see is the smile.

Wherever you are right now, God says, "I see you, and I'll fix you." God saw Hagar's brokenness and her potential. God loves you so deeply, there is nothing you should hide from Him. David said in Psalm 139:23–24, "Search me, O God, and know my heart; try me and know my anxious thoughts; and see if there be any hurtful way in me, and lead me in the everlasting way" (NASB). Go to God's well, and draw deep. He will satisfy your thirst. You may be single today, desiring to be married. Or maybe your marriage is in need of healing. You can go to the well and give it to God.

Provision at the well

Hagar went back to Abraham and Sarah. She humbled herself, and she gave birth to Ishmael. All seemed to be well. Fourteen years go by, and everything's going fine. Then God gave Abraham and Sarah the child of promise, Isaac.

> And the child grew, and was weaned: and Abraham made a great feast the same day that Isaac was weaned. And Sarah saw the son of Hagar the Egyptian, which she had born unto Abraham, mocking. Wherefore she said unto Abraham, Cast out this bondwoman and her son: for the son of this bondwoman shall not be heir with my son, even with Isaac....The thing was very grievous in Abraham's sight because of his son. And God said unto Abraham, Let it not be grievous in thy sight because of the lad, and because of thy bondwoman; in all that Sarah hath said unto thee, hearken unto her voice; for in Isaac shall thy seed be called. And

also of the son of the bondwoman will I make a
nation, because he is thy seed.
—GENESIS 21:8–10, 11–13

In this situation Hagar not only would have kept Abraham
from reaching his next level, but *her* next level would have
been affected as well. Sometimes God will separate you from
people. And it may not make sense at first, so you have to
examine your life to understand what God is doing. If you've
done everything right, if you've been obedient to what God
said—you've humbled yourself and submitted to authority—
and you now find yourself being pulled out of that relationship, God is up to something. He has a plan, just as He did
with Hagar.

God told her, "I have a plan for you, Hagar. You're going
to be OK. It's going to be all right." So we see that she got
up early in the morning and took some bread and a bottle
of water Abraham gave her, and she went with her son into
the wilderness.

But that water Abraham gave her didn't last forever. "And
the water was spent in the bottle, and she cast the child
under one of the shrubs" (Gen. 21:15). The water man gives
you won't last. It is only a temporary fix. Yet some of us are
looking to man to fill the voids in our lives. So we go to bed
with a man we aren't married to, hoping that will fill our
void, and the intimacy lasts only for five minutes. So you've
given yourself away, and you're still empty.

So often we seek anything and everything to meet our
needs. We spend money, we overeat, we get into ungodly
relationships—all so we can fill a void. But the satisfaction
is only temporary. Hagar's bottle was empty, "and she went,
and sat her down over against him a good way off, as it were

a bow shot: for she said, Let me not see the death of the child. And she sat over against him, and lift up her voice, and wept" (Gen. 21:16).

But then the Bible says, "God heard the voice of the lad" (Gen. 21:17). I love this passage of Scripture. I've taught it several times. When Hagar was by the well the first time, God sent an angel because He heard her. But now God hears *the lad*.

The Bible says:

> And the angel of God called to Hagar out of heaven, and said unto her, What aileth thee, Hagar? fear not; for God hath heard the voice of the lad where he is. Arise, lift up the lad, and hold him in thine hand; for I will make him a great nation. And God opened her eyes, and she saw a well of water; and she went, and filled the bottle with water, and gave the lad drink.
>
> —Genesis 21:17–19

When you are submitted to God's authority and find yourself in the wilderness, not understanding why you're being rejected, abandoned, or betrayed, your seed will begin to cry out to God. Your destiny will begin to cry out to God. Your potential will begin to cry out to God. And God will say, "I hear what I put on the inside of you, and I command it to come forth. What I have given you is there for a reason, and you can't die in the wilderness." Your seed may look puny, weak, and near death, but God hears its cry.

What is your seed? Is it your business? Is it your marriage? Is it your children? Is it your ministry? God hears the cry of your seed, and He's coming to nurture it. But notice this: God told Hagar to "lift up the lad, and hold him in thine hand." God is telling you the same thing. He saying, "I need you to pick up the seed and hold it up. I'm not going to do it for you. This is something I need you to do in faith. I need you to pick up the seed, hold it up, and let Me feed it." God wants you to do your part. He won't pick up the seed for you, but He will give it the sustenance it needs. Don't give up on your marriage; hold it up. Don't give up on your child; hold him up. Don't give up on that business; hold it up.

The Bible goes on to say, "And God was with the lad; and he grew, and dwelt in the wilderness, and became an archer" (Gen. 21:20). Hagar's seed flourished. And I believe she found joy. I believe she found happiness. I believe she got married again. I really do believe that.

Your blessing is at the well because that's where your source is.

Protection at the well

In 2 Samuel 17 we find a story of protection at a well:

> So the two of them left at once and went to the house of a man in Bahurim. He had a well in his courtyard, and they climbed down into it. His wife took a covering and spread it out over the opening of the well and scattered grain over it. No one knew anything about it.
> —2 SAMUEL 17:18–19, NIV

When David's spies came to this woman's house, she hid them in the well. Then when Absalom's servants went looking for them, they could not find them because they were covered in the well. Let me tell you, there's protection at the well.

We have power over all the power of the enemy, and when

we begin to pray, we can ask God to protect our loved ones. Instead of getting frustrated with them, instead of complaining about them, cover them. There's power in prayer.

Deliverance at the well

Of course, the most famous story in Scripture involving a well is the account of the Samaritan woman in John 4. When this woman arrived at the well, she was dry and empty. She had no water in her well. She put that smile on her face even though she was crying inside. And when she saw Jesus, she put on a religious attitude. But Jesus saw through her facade, and He spoke to her core. He knew how to get to the root issue.

In John 4:13–14 Jesus says to the Samaritan woman: "Everyone who drinks of this water will thirst again, but whoever drinks of the water that I shall give him will never thirst. Indeed, the water that I shall give him will become in him a well of water springing up into eternal life" (MEV).

The water Jesus spoke of could in no way be literal water. The Samaritan woman realized that, and she received what Jesus offered her, and she changed. And because she allowed God to change her at the well, God was able to use her to evangelize the whole town.

The puzzle pieces of your life are unique to you. My seven-year trial had many pieces that didn't make sense. Now looking back, I see God's mighty hand orchestrating a beautiful masterpiece. I believe that what I've learned can help you. Before He brought all the pieces together, I had to learn to love, endure, repent, walk in truth, and obey God's commands. God never does the work for you. He gives you the grace to do what He requires of you.

The puzzle pieces God allows in your life have everything

to do with what He wants to develop in you. God gives us everything we need to become the masterpieces He intended for us to be. I used the symbolism of the well as a practical teaching tool to show you that you can go to God for everything in your life. God is there to refresh, rebuild, rejuvenate, and restore you. He uses correction, prophecy, impartation, provision, protection, and deliverance. If you seek Him at the well, you will see Him bring together every puzzle piece in your life and create a picture that is beautiful to behold.

Chapter 10

STEP INTO
A NEW DIMENSION

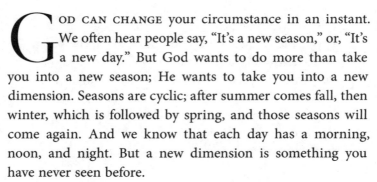

G OD CAN CHANGE your circumstance in an instant. We often hear people say, "It's a new season," or, "It's a new day." But God wants to do more than take you into a new season; He wants to take you into a new dimension. Seasons are cyclic; after summer comes fall, then winter, which is followed by spring, and those seasons will come again. And we know that each day has a morning, noon, and night. But a new dimension is something you have never seen before.

When Jesus came in contact with people—from the disciples to sinners to the Pharisees—He gave them insights they'd never received before. He made them see their future and their wrongdoing in a way they never had. He brought conviction and revelation that opened people's eyes to something new. That's what God does. We live in the finite, but God is infinite. He doesn't want to take us around the same block again and again. God wants to continually take us into new dimensions in Him.

Once I went to South Bend, Indiana, for a ministry engagement, and when I checked into the hotel, I was handed a letter at the front desk. It said, "Please be advised that at midnight the hotel will change ownership and transition from the South Bend Marriott to the DoubleTree by Hilton South Bend." So when I went to sleep, the hotel was Marriott, but when I woke up, it was DoubleTree. Though the transition I could not see probably had been in the works for several months, it seemed to happen overnight.

This is how it is with God. Although you may not see today what is happening in the spirit, God is at work on your behalf. Always be ready for God to move. He can cause your situation to change overnight.

The Bible says:

> Forget the former things; do not dwell on the past.
> See, I am doing a new thing! Now it springs up;
> do you not perceive it? I am making a way in the
> wilderness and streams in the wasteland. The wild
> animals honor me, the jackals and the owls, because
> I provide water in the wilderness and streams in the
> wasteland, to give drink to my people, my chosen.
> —ISAIAH 43:18–20, NIV

God desires that we come into the new. In verse 18 of Isaiah 43, God says, "Forget the former things; do not dwell on the past" (NIV). These words originally were meant to comfort a people in captivity. God's chosen people were going to be brought in exile to the wicked nation of Babylon. During their time in captivity, they probably reminisced about the good old days. I imagine they remembered how God rescued them from Egypt, parted the Red Sea, and defeated all the nations that kept them from entering the Promised Land.

When comparing those times with their season of captivity, they probably thought, "Those were the days!"[1]

As Christians we do the same thing. We reminisce about the good times in the past. But God says, "Do not dwell on the past. See, I am doing a new thing! Now it springs up; do you not perceive it?" (vv. 18–19). God was telling the people that the wonderful stories of the past were nothing in comparison with what He was about to do!

This was an amazing promise because it meant God was going to rescue them again. He said, "I am making a way in the wilderness and streams in the wasteland" (v. 19). God's children were imprisoned in a country that was surrounded by desert wasteland. They were utterly hopeless because even if they escaped from Babylon, there was absolutely nowhere for them to go. They would meet certain death in the wasteland. So God declared that He would put streams in the desert wastelands! God was preparing them for the impossible—He was preparing a highway for them to walk on. He was going to provide water for them as they journeyed back to the Promised Land.

God said in verse 20, "The wild animals honor me, the jackals and the owls." That is such a powerful statement.

Just as God's people felt trapped, many of us have been in situations where there seemed to be no way out. Some people feel trapped in their marriages, jobs, ministry, bodies, or just life itself. That is no way to live. Jesus said He came to give us life and that we might have it more abundantly (John 10:10)! God wants you to step into a new dimension of life.

When you go see a 3-D movie, you wear special glasses to get the optimal effect. Without the 3-D glasses the movie looks cloudy and unclear. But with the 3-D glasses the movie comes alive, and you feel almost as if the picture is in your lap. Well, I imagine God wants to give you spiritual 3-D glasses so you can see life more clearly and focus on what He has for you. God wants you to be passionate about your purpose and even more passionate about Him. Your next dimension will unfold more of His plans for your life.

Get Rid of the Old

One of the first principles we see for moving into a new dimension is to forget the old. That means we must focus on neither our victories nor our failures. We mustn't get so entangled with the past that we hinder our future. Jesus said:

> And no one puts new wine into old wineskins. If he does, the new wine will burst the skins and it will be spilled, and the skins will be destroyed. But new wine must be put into fresh wineskins.
>
> —Luke 5:37–38, esv

Obviously this is a biblical principle. Jesus is telling us that in order to get something new, we first have to get rid of the old.

Starting over was a difficult task for me. I had previously planted a church with my husband, but back then the world was a much smaller place without social media. There were many things we pioneered in Central Florida that hadn't been done by a young African American couple. We stood as a team and pastored together; we were on radio, television, and billboards; we built a building from the ground up; and we became a large church in a few short years without the backing of a denomination or church network. When God led me to start Majestic Life, things were different. What was new before was old now. So I couldn't bring the old way of doing things into the new. I had to hear from God about how to launch a ministry.

The last time, we built our ministry through traditional media and advertisement. This time God told me not to advertise. Honestly that word was not too difficult for me to obey because I wasn't thrilled about pastoring again. But I wanted to be obedient to the Lord. God did exactly what He said He would do. We outgrew our facility in the first three years.

It is easy to fall back into our comfort zones of the past when God wants to do something new. Jesus said, "No one after drinking old wine wants the new, for they say, 'The old is better'" (Luke 5:39, NIV). If God is moving you into something new, the old isn't better. It's familiar. That's why it's so easy to justify falling back into it. What is familiar is comfortable, but God wants us to be led by His Spirit. The old and the new cannot be utilized together. You cannot combine them without destroying both.

You may have heard the story of a young woman who was cooking a pot roast for her new husband. He watched her as she cut off the end of the pot roast before putting it in the pan. When her husband asked why she cut off the end of the pot roast, she chuckled and said, "I don't know. My mother always did it that way, and that's how I've always done it." It turns out her mother always did it that way because her pan was too small for a regular-size pot roast, so she had to cut off the ends so it would fit.

If we are not discerning, we may find ourselves doing things because that's how we've always done them and not because that is what God is leading us to do. God says, "Don't get comfortable. Get out of your comfort zone, and go to the next dimension of your purpose."

Again, Luke 5:39 says, "No man also having drunk old

wine straightway desireth new: for he saith, The old is better." In other words, the new wine may not be as smooth to the palate as the aged wine. The new may taste sharp, so you may not want it. Life can be like that. We have some things that are our "old faithfuls"—they may include a pair of comfy slippers, an old recliner, a favorite college sweater, or an old pair of jeans. They are your favorite because they are comfortable and they fit just right. The newer jeans are harder and tighter. So you always go for the comfortable, older pair in your closet. But God says that to go into this new dimension, you must be open to His will for your life. We can't turn to the same people, same food, or same routine just because it's familiar.

The principle of getting rid of the old so God can do something new was first introduced at Shiloh. God established the city of Shiloh during the time of the judges, and it became the center of all religious activity in Israel. Shiloh is where God spoke to His people.[2]

While Eli was high priest, the Israelites went to battle with the Philistines and were defeated. Surprised by the loss, they decided to send to Shiloh to bring the ark of the covenant with them to battle so they would have victory. But instead the Israelites again were defeated, and the Philistines captured the ark. Shocked once again by this loss, a messenger ran to Shiloh to tell Eli what had happened.

> And the messenger...said [to Eli], Israel is fled before the Philistines, and there hath been also a great slaughter among the people, and thy two sons also, Hophni and Phinehas, are dead, and the ark of God is taken. And it came to pass, when he made mention of the ark of God, that [Eli] fell from off the seat backward by the side of the gate, and his

neck brake, and he died: for he was an old man, and heavy. And he had judged Israel forty years. And his daughter in law, Phinehas' wife, was with child, near to be delivered: and when she heard the tidings that the ark of God was taken, and that her father in law and her husband were dead, she bowed herself and travailed; for her pains came upon her. And about the time of her death the women that stood by her said unto her, Fear not; for thou hast born a son. But she answered not, neither did she regard it. And she named the child Ichabod, saying, The glory is departed from Israel: because the ark of God was taken, and because of her father in law and her husband. And she said, The glory is departed from Israel: for the ark of God is taken.

—1 SAMUEL 4:17–22

God is long-suffering, but He is also holy. The Israelites were suffering defeat because they had allowed wickedness and idol worship to desecrate God's temple. (See 1 Samuel 3.) God would not and could not allow that, and He removed His presence from Israel. Today the same principle holds true. Of course, not all churches have gone the way of the world, but there is a lot of ambition in Western church culture. Too many ministries are more driven by money and fame than by a desire to reach lost souls and see people mature in Christ.

Israel had stopped putting the Lord at the center of the nation. The Israelites had become dull in their worship. The temple priests disregarded the sacredness of their duties and the holiness of the temple. As a result, God spoke a word of correction through the prophet Jeremiah:

Thus saith the LORD of hosts, the God of Israel, Amend your ways and your doings, and I will cause you to dwell in this place. Trust ye not in lying words, saying, The temple of the LORD, the temple of the LORD, the temple of the LORD, are these. For if ye throughly amend your ways and your doings…then will I cause you to dwell in this place, in the land that I gave to your fathers, for ever and ever. Behold, ye trust in lying words, that cannot profit. Will ye steal, murder, and commit adultery, and swear falsely, and burn incense unto Baal, and walk after other gods whom ye know not; and come and stand before me in this house, which is called by my name, and say, We are delivered to do all these abominations? Is this house, which is called by my name, become a den of robbers in your eyes? Behold, even I have seen it, saith the LORD. But go ye now unto my place which was in Shiloh, where I set my name at the first, and see what I did to it for the wickedness of my people Israel.…Therefore will I do unto this house, which is called by my name, wherein ye trust, and unto the place which I gave to you and to your fathers, as I have done to Shiloh.
—JEREMIAH 7:3–5, 7–12, 14

God had heard the people. They were thinking, "The Lord can't destroy this temple. It's His everlasting house. It holds our history and traditions. Look at all these majestic buildings. He'll never abandon what He has established here." But God was serious, and that's why He warned them that He was not going to tolerate their wickedness.

I can hear people today saying, "I am on television," "We just built this huge edifice," "Everyone knows my name," "I am the head of the finance committee," and "People love to hear me preach." But God will not tolerate sin. We serve a long-suffering, wonderful God who wishes no one would perish. He is faithful to warn us before He brings judgment. He always gives us an opportunity to repent.

Many people don't realize the captain of *Titanic* received six warnings about drifting ice before the ship's catastrophic crash into an iceberg on April 14, 1912. The first warning came at 9:00 a.m. from RMS *Caronia*, which reported icebergs, growlers, and field ice. The captain acknowledged receipt of the message. Then, at 1:42 p.m., the steamship *Baltic* relayed a report from the Greek ship *Athenia* that she had been "passing icebergs and large quantities of field ice." The captain acknowledged this also and showed the report to J. Bruce Ismay, the chairman of the White Star Line of Liverpool, England, who was aboard the *Titanic* for her maiden voyage. Then, at 1:45 p.m., the German ship SS *Amerika* reported that she had "passed two large icebergs." This message never reached the captain or the other officers on the *Titanic*.

The steamship *Californian* reported three large icebergs at 7:30 p.m., and at 9:40 p.m. the steamer *Mesaba* reported: "Saw much heavy pack ice and great number large icebergs. Also field ice." This message too never left the *Titanic*'s radio room. A final warning was received at about 11:00 p.m. from the *Californian*, which had stopped for the night in an ice field several miles away, but Jack Phillips, the *Titanic*'s senior wireless operator, cut it off and signaled back: "Shut up! Shut up! I'm working Cape Race." Although the crew was aware of ice in the vicinity, the ship's speed was not reduced, and it continued to move at a rapid pace because they wanted to reach their destination on time.[3]

We can learn a major lesson from the *Titanic* crew's failure to heed the warnings that would have saved lives and the ship. God's grace is sufficient, but it will not be frustrated. There are spiritual principles and laws that are set in motion when we step outside of God's protection. Oftentimes we think God is keeping record of every action we take. Technically He is because He is omniscient. But more realistically what we experience is the fact that He set certain principles in motion. The wages of sin is death. Every action has a consequence. God loves us so much that He warns us when we get off track to save us from the consequences of certain behavior. However, if we choose to ignore God's warnings, then we will suffer the consequences.

Jesus invited everyone to accept Him. He called out to the Gentile and the Jew alike, the lost and the religious. He wished all would come to the saving knowledge of Christ. Anyone could receive healing, forgiveness, and salvation if he believed. But the religious crowd refused His offer. So Christ testified of them:

> O Jerusalem, Jerusalem, thou that killest the prophets, and stonest them which are sent unto thee, how often would I have gathered thy children together, even as a hen gathereth her chickens under her wings, and ye would not! Behold, your house is left unto you desolate. [In other words, this temple is now your house, not Mine. I'm gone.] For I say unto you, Ye shall not see me henceforth, till ye shall say, Blessed is he that cometh in the name of the Lord.
>
> —MATTHEW 23:37–39

Jesus was saying, "Go have your beautiful edifices, great choirs, huge congregations, and great social status. But you are going to have to do it without Me."

That is exactly what happened in Jeremiah 7. The people continued to worship without God. Crowds still came to the temple, but God's presence was no longer there. God sent prophets to warn the Israelites of their sin, but they refused to listen.

God does not just want His bride immaculate on the outside; she must be immaculate from the inside out.

In Jeremiah 7:12 God instructed the children of Israel: "Go ye now unto my place which was in Shiloh, where I set my name at the first, and see what I did to it for the wickedness of my people Israel [and now I'm about to do it again]."

He was telling them, "You're just like Shiloh. You've allowed sin and corruption in My house. I'm about to remove My glory from your midst."

Jeremiah 7:16 stands out to me; in it God says, "Therefore pray not thou for this people, neither lift up cry nor prayer for them, neither make intercession to me: for I will not hear thee." He was saying: "Don't bother praying for this old work. It's dead and gone. There is no more hope." God was doing away with the old system.

In Ezekiel 14 certain elders came to the prophet to inquire of the Lord. They wanted to know what God was saying to His people. But the Lord told Ezekiel, "These men have set up their idols in their heart, and put the stumblingblock of their iniquity before their face: should I be enquired of at all by them?" (Ezek. 14:3). He was saying, in other words: "They've come here as if they're truly seeking Me. But they're hiding wicked idols in their hearts. Why should I answer them?"

How can we step into a new dimension when we are carrying old idols in our heart? Idol worship is not merely the worship of a statue or figurine; it's a mind-set and a heart issue.

Sadly today many Christians measure their self-worth by

their popularity, position in ministry, career, possessions, or paycheck. Some people, pastors and laypersons alike, believe their peers determine how successful they are. Some pastors base their success in ministry on how many members they have, how large their buildings are, and how much money is in their budget. God is once again saying in our day, "I will destroy and devour every ministry that's of flesh or that's filled with hype and materialism. And I'm going to raise up shepherds after My own heart." (See Isaiah 42:16.)

A Heavenly Perspective

Jesus wants His followers to live in a new dimension, a place they have never dwelt in before. He wants to take us to this place so we can experience abundant life. A dimension is a measurable degree or limit to which something can be extended.[4] In Ephesians 3:18–19 the apostle Paul talked about the dimensions of God's love for us, saying, "May be able to comprehend with all saints what is the breadth, and length, and depth, and height; and to know the love of Christ, which passeth knowledge, that ye might be filled with all the fulness of God."

When God did away with the old temple worship, He led us to Pentecost and moved the followers of Jesus to a new dimension of life, to a place they had never experienced before that moment. Jesus often did that with people. He caused them to think about life from a vantage point they'd never had before that point in time.

While living in exile on the Isle of Patmos, the apostle John experienced a new dimension. He wrote:

> After this I looked, and, behold, a door was opened
> in heaven: and the first voice which I heard was as

it were of a trumpet talking with me; which said,
Come up hither, and I will shew thee things which
must be hereafter. And immediately I was in the
spirit: and, behold, a throne was set in heaven, and
one sat on the throne.

—REVELATION 4:1–2

Before we go further, I want to direct your attention to
the word *looked*. This reminds us that we must seek before
we can find. Jesus is coming back for those who are looking
for Him. There are several instances in Scripture where the
door of heaven was opened, and someone received a vision
of the heavens—the prophet Ezekiel, Daniel, and Stephen in
the New Testament, just to name a few. God is not the one
putting the limits on; we do that to ourselves. In Revelation
4:1 the voice said, "Come up hither." That voice is still beckoning us to "come up hither." Focus your attention heaven-
ward, not on the things of this earth. Jesus's call always has
been for us to come to Him.

In the Revelation, Jesus the Voice tells John why he must
come up hither: so He can show John "things which must
be hereafter." John would be given a glimpse into the future.
John could have had a vision of this, or he could have been
transported into heaven for a moment to see all of this. We
do not know exactly how the revelation was given to John.
What we do know is that when we view something from
earth, we see just the here and now. When we see something from a heavenly viewpoint, we can see yesterday and
tomorrow.

When John saw into heaven, this is what he witnessed:

And before the throne there was a sea of glass like
unto crystal: and in the midst of the throne, and

round about the throne, were four beasts full of
eyes before and behind. And the first beast was like
a lion, and the second beast like a calf, and the third
beast had a face as a man, and the fourth beast was
like a flying eagle.

—REVELATION 4:6–7

John was on the island of Patmos, and yet He was still
able to see into heaven. He actually may have been translated
into a new dimension of glory for a period of time. He was
in exile, so his environment was free of external voices. In
that setting John must have saturated himself in God. This
reveals a key to moving to a new dimension: walking closely
with God.

The Book of Genesis tells us that God's relationship with
Adam and Eve was so close He walked daily with them in
the garden (Gen. 3:8). It's clear that He created mankind for
His enjoyment and companionship. We read later in Genesis
that Enoch walked so closely with God that "he was not; for
God took him" (Gen. 5:24). Now that is an intimate relationship with God. Enoch didn't die; God just translated him
into heaven. Enoch stepped into a new dimension with God
because of his intimacy with Him.

God wants us to have that same closeness with Him.
He wants us all to step into a new dimension by first com-
muning with Him.

By faith Enoch was translated that he should not see
death; and was not found, because God had translated him: for before his translation he had this testimony, that he pleased God. But without faith it is
impossible to please him: for he that cometh to God

must believe that he is, and that he is a rewarder of them that diligently seek him.

—HEBREWS 11:5–6

God will reward us when we diligently seek Him.

When you walk with God, you will receive revelation from Him. God warned Enoch of the great flood that was to come and destroy the entire earth. We know this because Genesis 5:21 says Enoch begat Methuselah after he had lived sixty-five years. The name Methuselah means "his death shall bring."[5] God likely told Enoch of the great disaster that was to come, and his son became a prophetic sign of that terrible event. Methuselah, in turn, must have warned Noah, for we read in Hebrews 11:7, "By faith Noah, being warned of God of things not seen as yet, moved with fear, prepared an ark to the saving of his house; by the which he condemned the world, and became heir of the righteousness which is by faith."

Enoch not only prophesied God's judgment in Noah's day; he prophesied Jesus's return:

> And Enoch also, the seventh from Adam, prophesied of these, saying, Behold, the Lord cometh with ten thousands of his saints, to execute judgment upon all, and to convince all that are ungodly among them of all their ungodly deeds which they have ungodly committed, and of all their hard speeches which ungodly sinners have spoken against him.
>
> —JUDE 14–15

I get chills every time I read that passage!

Enoch received this word from the Lord in another dimension. And he was able to receive this kind of revelation

191

because Enoch knew how to walk with God. I believe Enoch was so passionate in warning everyone about the flood that his son Lamech must have gotten an earful. Lamech died five years before the flood, but he must have been the one to share Enoch's message with his son Noah. I believe that Noah was able to stand the scrutiny of those around him because he was confident his grandfather Enoch had heard from God. Noah was the tenth generation from Adam, and his family had a history of walking with God.

The wisdom of God is everlasting. The Bible says, "Yet we do speak wisdom among those spiritually mature [believers who have teachable hearts and a greater understanding]; but [it is a higher] wisdom not [the wisdom] of this present age nor of the rulers and leaders of this age, who are passing away" (1 Cor. 2:6, AMP).

In this verse the apostle Paul declares that the wisdom of God is "not...of this present age nor of the rulers...of this age, who are passing away." When I was in elementary school, I was fascinated by the planets. I memorized them in order: Mercury, Venus, Earth, Mars, Jupiter, Saturn, Uranus, Neptune, and Pluto. Well, now we are being told Pluto is not a planet but a star. The wisdom of man is forever changing. When I gave birth to my oldest daughter, our pediatrician instructed us to lay her on her side to nap and sleep. By the time I had my third child, mothers were being told to lay babies on their backs.

However, God's wisdom isn't temporal like man's wisdom. God's wisdom is eternal (Isa. 40:8, AMP). And it reveals His truth to us (1 Cor. 2:7).

God wants us to go higher. We read in Revelation 4 that He told John, "Come up hither" (v. 1); now this scripture says God predestined "our glory." God is reminding us that we go from glory to glory. The more we remain in His glory, the more it affects our lives and moves us into a greater dimension in Him.

We have many self-help gurus to choose from nowadays. It is possible to get certified in life coaching in a matter of weeks. We look to people with charisma, education, and influence to teach us how to be like them. We try to glean from them. But the Word warns us not to get enticed by the wisdom of men. God wants us to be supernatural, not superficial. The wisdom of God takes us to another dimension.

REST AND PEACE

One of the most exciting aspects of the new dimension is that it allows us to experience a supernatural manifestation of the rest and peace of God. Zechariah 8:11–12 (NKJV) says:

> "But now I will not treat the remnant of this people as in the former days," says the LORD of hosts. "For the seed shall be prosperous, the vine shall give its fruit, the ground shall give her increase, and the heavens shall give their dew—I will cause the remnant of this people to possess all these."

This passage reminds me that God is with the remnant; He is promising blessings to His last days' remnant church. New-dimension thinking allows us to see our puzzle pieces through the Spirit. God is not conventional; He lives outside of man's dimension. He wants us to come up so we can see His power in our lives. You may be the underdog, and all odds are against you. Don't be discouraged. God promises His remnant four things in Zechariah 8:

- "The seed shall be prosperous."

- "The vine shall give its fruit."

- "The ground shall give her increase."

- "The heavens shall give their dew."

If this is what God promises His remnant, you may be wondering what a remnant is. When I was growing up, we spoke of carpet or fabric remnants; those were the leftovers, the fragments, pieces at the end of a roll that had little value. The remnant in Zechariah 8 is not the end of a thing; it is actually a new beginning. The remnant is where God pours His favor and anointing for the future of His people and His church. Moses and Enoch were part of remnants that did not compromise God's Word, and as a result God supernaturally blessed them, and they received a great wisdom and promotion to their next dimension.

The four promises in Zechariah 8 are pretty self-explanatory except for the promise that the heavens shall give their dew. What exactly is dew? It refers to the tiny drops of water that often appear on plants and blades of grass early in the morning. As one source explained:

> The dew point is the temperature at which moisture in the air begins to condense. Objects receive heat from the sun during the day by the direct process of radiation. But, when night comes, the blade of grass is not able to retain the heat that is stored during the day. So, the little grass becomes cool. Also, the air around it becomes cool as well. Then, when the air reaches the dew point, it can no longer hold all the moisture that's present in the air, and so it deposits this excess moisture as dew on the blade of grass.[6]

All this happens before the sun warms up the day and evaporation takes place. But this dew provides nourishment to grass and vegetation for the entire day. I did an extensive search on the references to *dew* in Scripture, and I found some interesting truths that parallel our journey to step into a new dimension.

Dew comes in stillness.

Dew in the natural comes only in the still of the morning. Psalm 46:10 says, "Be still, and know that I am God: I will be exalted among the heathen, I will be exalted in the earth." The phrase "be still" in this text means to cease from striving. If you cease from striving and know that God is your provider and protection, you can receive heavenly dew. Just as natural dew brings nourishment to the vegetation in the stillness of the morning, so does heavenly dew bring nourishment to our souls and spirits through the presence of the Lord.

Isaiah 30:15 says we shall receive strength "in quietness and in confidence" (MEV). You don't get direction in the midst of strife, commotion, doubt, and striving. Your nourishment comes in quietness and confidence in God. First Kings 19:12 says, "And after the earthquake a fire; but the LORD was not in the fire: and after the fire a still small voice." So many of us miss God because we are looking for Him in the noise of life. He wants your faith to be in what you can't see or hear in the natural; He wants it to be in what you hear in your spirit.

When I learned how to be still and cease striving, God's grace overwhelmed me. It was as Proverbs 19:12 says: "The king's wrath is as the roaring of a lion; but his favour is as dew upon the grass." Doors of opportunity opened that I desired but didn't seek. I felt a renewed vitality as I let go and let God. God desires to make us whole, but we must totally depend on Him by faith.

Dew reveals provision.

In Scripture the dew reveals provision. We see this in the blessing Isaac prayed over Jacob in Genesis 27:28–29:

> Therefore may God give you of the dew of heaven, of the fatness of the earth, and plenty of grain and wine. Let peoples serve you, and nations bow down to you. Be master over your brethren, and let your mother's sons bow down to you. Cursed be everyone who curses you, and blessed be those who bless you!
> —GENESIS 27:28–29, NKJV

And we see a similar connection between the dew and God's provision in Numbers 11:7–9, when manna fell from heaven on top of the dew. Manna fell from heaven every morning, and the children of Israel were not allowed to store it up because God declared that maggots and worms would eat it if it was kept. (See Exodus 16.) God wanted to be their daily bread. That is also His desire for you! He wants you to lean on Him for your every need.

Dew protects.

The Bible tells us that dew gives us protection and power over our enemies! Look at Deuteronomy 33:28–29 (NKJV):

> Then Israel shall dwell in safety, the fountain of Jacob alone, in a land of grain and new wine; His heavens shall also drop dew. Happy are you, O Israel! Who is like you, a people saved by the LORD, the shield of your help and the sword of your majesty! Your

enemies shall submit to you, and you shall tread down their high places.

God's heavenly dew is His anointing on your life to destroy every yoke of the enemy. You can obtain the spiritual dew of God by cultivating an intimate relationship with Him through prayer and worship.

However, God's heavenly dew is withheld when there is disobedience, as the prophet Haggai declared:

> "You expected much, but see, it turned out to be little. What you brought home, I blew away. Why?" declares the LORD Almighty. "Because of my house, which remains a ruin, while each of you is busy with your own house. Therefore, because of you the heavens have withheld their dew and the earth its crops."
>
> —HAGGAI 1:9–10, NIV

Dew is temporary.

The dew is not permanent; it's for a season. Isaiah 55:6 tells us to "seek the LORD while He may be found, call you upon Him while He is near" (MEV). Seasons come and go. So we must not get stuck in an old move of God or a comfort zone. God provided for Elijah by causing ravens to bring him food and supplying water from a brook. (See 1 Kings 17:2–6.) But the season came when the brook dried up and Elijah had to move forward to another location. I often see believers stuck in a dried-up, old move of God where fruit is no longer being produced. I wanted to stay by the brook. I wanted my husband. I wanted my New Destiny church family. I wanted my home. But they were all gone. I had to move forward.

In Galatians 6:9 Paul says, "Let us not grow weary while doing good, for in due season we shall reap if we do not lose heart" (NKJV). The dew season empowers you for the *do* season so you can walk in your due season!

The dew season is your time with God. During your dew time with God He heals your brokenness, empowers you, and prepares you for your *do* season. I started Majestic Life after spending time with God in prayer and hearing His voice during my dew time. Once God gives you some direction, start moving toward what He has for you. *Do* something. God needs your faith to agree with your actions. "Faith without works is dead" (James 2:26, NKJV). If you want to own a business, start by writing a business plan. Just *do* something besides talk about it.

When I started to *do* something after my *dew* time with God, I began to walk in my due season.

- My due season came when God blessed my network marketing business. The only reason I started the business was because I lost everything in divorce.

- My due season came when my church was able to provide a salary for me after its third anniversary. I hadn't received any income from the church for two years prior.

- My due season came when my legal battles were over and a settlement was reached for the children's inheritance.

- My due season came when my first book, *When It All Falls Apart*, was published.

- My due season came when I was asked to be the radio announcer for the gospel programming on Cox Media's FM station Star 94.5.

- My due season came when I started a record label and our song "So Amazing" went national.

- My due season came when Majestic Life moved into its own facility.

- My due season came when I paid off my home.

- My due season came when my children graduated from high school and went on to college.

It's true—the difficult times prepared me for the increase.

It's hard to believe now that I once thought the discombobulated puzzle pieces I experienced in those seven years had no rhyme or reason. In some ways I felt that life always would be a series of difficulties. I'd almost gotten used to the pressure of one trial after another. Paradoxically God used each unpleasant puzzle piece and brought all the pieces together for a beautiful purpose.

NOT EASILY BROKEN

When they all come together, life's many puzzle pieces all seem to make sense. When the picture on your box comes to fruition, every piece of your puzzle becomes more precious and valuable to you than you ever expected. You realize that every piece of your puzzle, even the unattractive ones, was necessary to complete the picture God had in mind for you.

The rhyme is one of the most popular devices in the English language. The most famous modern rhyme is:

Humpty Dumpty sat on a wall,
Humpty Dumpty had a great fall.
All the king's horses and all the king's men
Couldn't put Humpty together again.

How true is this? People can never put you back together after you've been broken to pieces. Only the King of kings and Lord of lords has that capability. Allow God to put you back together again. And when it all comes together, you will not be broken easily.

NOTES

Chapter 1: Puzzled

1. *Oxford Living Dictionaries*, s.v. "sovereign," accessed October 27, 2016, http://www.oxforddictionaries.com/us /definition/american_english/sovereign.

Chapter 2: This Is Not What I Expected

1. "Church Members Protest Pastor Tims' Replacement," WFTV, updated December 23, 2011, accessed October 27, 2016, http://www.wftv.com/news/local/members-megachurch-protest -pastor-tims-replacement/286561116; Vincent Funaro, "Zachery Tims' New Destiny Members Rally Against Paula White Succession," *The Christian Post*, December 23, 2011, accessed October 27, 2016, http://www.christianpost.com/news/zachery-tims-new -destiny-members-rally-against-paula-white-succession-65615/; Jeff Kunerth, "New Destiny Christian Center Members Protesting Paula; They Want Riva," *The Church Lady* (blog), accessed October 27, 2016, http://thechurchladyblogs.com/new-destiny -christian-center-members-protesting-paula-they-want-riva/; Jennifer LeClaire, "Amid Protests, Paula White Named Senior Pastor of Zachery Tims' Church," *Charisma News*, December 29, 2011, accessed October 27, 2016, http://www.charismanews.com /us/32580-amid-protests-paula-white-named-senior-pastor -of-zachery-tims-church; Scott McDonnell, "Outrage Over Possible Replacement for Pastor Zachary Tims," *Bay News 9*, December 20, 2011, accessed October 27, 2016, http://www .baynews9.com/content/news/baynews9/news/article.html/content /news/articles/ot/both/2011/12/20/Outrage_over_possible _replacement_for_Pastor_Zachary_Tims.html.

2. *Oxford Living Dictionaries*, s.v. "earthquake," accessed October 27, 2016,https://en.oxforddictionaries.com/definition/us /earthquake.

3. Blue Letter Bible, s.v. "redeem," accessed October 27, 2016, https://www.blueletterbible.org/lang/Lexicon/Lexicon.cfm ?strongs=G1805&t=KJV.

4. Blue Letter Bible, s.v. "*kairos*," accessed October 27, 2016, https://www.blueletterbible.org/lang/Lexicon/Lexicon.cfm ?strongs=G2540&t=KJV.

Chapter 3: The Tapestry of Life

1. Tim Challies, "God's Tapestry," January 19, 2015, accessed August 24, 2016, http://www.challies.com/articles/gods-tapestry.

2. Dictionary.com, s.v. "enmity," accessed October 27, 2016, http://www.dictionary.com/browse/enmity.

3. Hamil R. Harris, "D.C. Judge Reinstates Joel Peebles to Board of Jericho City of Praise Church," *The Washington Post*, July 7, 2015, accessed October 27, 2016, https://www .washingtonpost.com/local/dc-judge-reinstates-joel-peebles-to -board-of-jericho-city-of-praise-church/2015/07/07/b049064c -24d5-11e5-b72c-2b7d516e1e0e_story.html; Hamil R. Harris, "Peebles Returns to Jericho City of Praise," *The Washington Post*, August 15, 2015, accessed October 27, 2016, https://www .washingtonpost.com/news/local/wp/2015/08/14/jericho/.

4. *Merriam-Webster's Collegiate Dictionary*, eleventh edition (Springfield, MA: Merriam-Webster Inc., 2003), s.v. "fallow."

5. Bible Encyclopedia, "Fallow-ground," accessed October 27, 2016, http://christiananswers.net/dictionary/fallow-ground.html.

Chapter 4: Embracing the Dreaded Puzzle Pieces

1. Charles Stanley, "What Happened to Paul in the Desert?," Jesus.org, accessed October 27, 2016, http://www.jesus.org/early -church-history/the-apostle-paul/what-happened-to-paul-in-the -desert.html.

2. *Merriam-Webster's Collegiate Dictionary*, eleventh edition (Springfield, MA: Merriam-Webster Inc., 2003), s.v. "tribulation," "distress," "persecution," "famine," "nakedness," "peril," "sword."

3. "The Meaning of 'More Than Conquerors,'" Christianity Rediscovered, July 3, 2009, accessed October 27, 2017, http:// christianity-rediscovered.blogspot.com/2009/07/meaning-of-more -than-conquerors.html.

4. Bible Hub, "Micah 4:10," accessed October 27, 2016, http://biblehub.com/commentaries/micah/4-10.htm.

CHAPTER 5: DEFINING MOMENTS

1. Greg Carr, "A Defining Moment," SermonCentral, February 2011, accessed Oct. 20, 2016, http://www.sermoncentral.com/print_friendly.asp?SermonID=154241.

2. Patrick McCrann, "How to Beat the Wall During Your Marathon," Active.com, accessed October 20, 2016, http://www.active.com/running/articles/how-to-beat-the-wall-during-your-marathon?page=3.

3. Jennifer LeClaire, "Why Are So Many Pastors Committing Suicide?," *Charisma News*, December 11, 2013, accessed October 20, 2016, http://www.charismanews.com/opinion/watchman-on-the-wall/42063-why-are-so-many-pastors-committing-suicide.

CHAPTER 6: GOD WILL RESTORE

1. *Merriam-Webster's Collegiate Dictionary*, eleventh edition (Springfield, MA: Merriam-Webster Inc., 2003), s.v. "reproach."

2. *Merriam-Webster's Collegiate Dictionary*, eleventh edition (Springfield, MA: Merriam-Webster Inc., 2003), s.v. "storm."

3. *Merriam-Webster's Collegiate Dictionary*, eleventh edition (Springfield, MA: Merriam-Webster Inc., 2003), s.v. "maneuver."

CHAPTER 7: KEEP MOVING FORWARD

1. *Merriam-Webster's Collegiate Dictionary*, eleventh edition (Springfield, MA: Merriam-Webster Inc., 2003), s.v. "restrain."

2. Bible Hub, accessed October 24, 2016, http://biblehub.com/greek/1398.htm.

3. "How Long Was Joseph in Potiphar's House? How Long in Prison?," The Amazing Bible Timeline, June 29, 2013, accessed October 24, 2016, https://amazingbibletimeline.com/blog/q27_joseph_how_long_in_prison/.

4. Allan Turner, "A Study of the Book of Ephesians," re:thinking, November 23, 1998, accessed November 17, 2016, http://www.allanturner.com/eph_6.html.

CHAPTER 8: DOUBLE HONOR FOR YOUR SHAME

1. "God Is at Work–The Story of Ruth Part II," Discover the Word, September 8, 2010, accessed October 25, 2016, https://discovertheword.org/2010/09/08/the-old-testament-word-hesed-and-the-profound-meaning-it-has-for-us-today/.

2. Rifat Sonsino, "On the Book of Ruth," ReformJudaism.org, accessed October 25, 2016, http://www.reformjudaism.org/book-ruth.

3. Rabbi Dovid Rosenfeld, "Ruth vs. Orpah: The High Stakes of Life," Aish.com, accessed October 25, 2016, http://www.aish.com/h/sh/t/Ruth-vs-Orpah-The-High-Stakes-of-Life.html.

4. Strong's Hebrew Lexicon, s.v. "H7531–ritspah," Blue Letter Bible, accessed October 25, 2016, https://www.blueletterbible.org/lang/lexicon/lexicon.cfm?Strongs=H7531.

5. *Merriam-Webster's Learner's Dictionary*, s.v. "endurance," accessed October 25, 2016, http://www.merriam-webster.com/dictionary/endurance.

CHAPTER 9: DON'T RUN FROM GOD

1. A special thanks to Pastor Fred Markes for his insights into Jonah in his sermon "On the Run," SermonCentral.com, October 2009, accessed October 25, 2016, http://www.sermoncentral.com/sermons/on-the-run-fred-markes-sermon-on-jonah-140962.asp.

CHAPTER 10: STEP INTO A NEW DIMENSION

1. Some of these insights originally were shared by David Wilkerson in "God Is Doing a New Thing in His Church," accessed October 25, 2016, http://www.ldolphin.org/newthing.html.

2. David Wilkerson, "God Is Doing a New Thing in His Church," accessed October 25, 2016, http://www.ldolphin.org/newthing.html.

3. Paul R. Ryan, ed., Oceanus: *The International Magazine of Marine Science and Policy*, Volume 28, Number 4, Winter 185/86, accessed October 27, 2016, https://archive.org/stream/oceanusv2804wood/oceanusv2804wood_djvu.txt; see also Awesome Stories, "Titanic—The Fatal Voyage—Ice Warnings Ignored," accessed October 25, 2016, https://www.awesomestories.com

/asset/view/ICE-WARNINGS-IGNORED-Fatal-Voyage-The
-Titanic.

4. *Merriam-Webster's Learner's Dictionary*, s.v. "dimension,"
accessed October 27, 2016, http://www.merriam-webster.com
/dictionary/dimension.

5. Chuck Missler, "Meanings of the Names in Genesis 5," Koi-
nonia House, accessed October 27, 2016, http://www.khouse.org
/articles/2000/284/.

6. Kevin Taylor, "It's Dew Time," SermonCentral.com,
accessed October 27, 2016, http://www.sermoncentral.com
/sermons/its-dew-time-kevin-taylor-sermon-on-gods-provision
-31373.asp; see also *Encyclopædia Britannica Online*, s.v. "dew,"
accessed October 27, 2016, https://www.britannica.com/science
/dew.

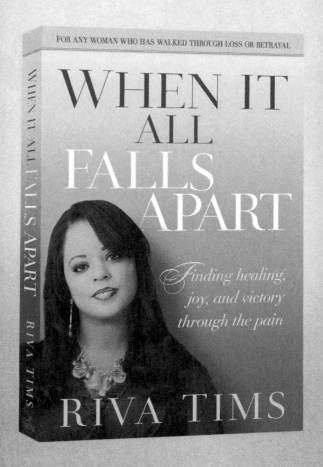

CONNECT WITH US!